KEEP

THOSE FEET

MOVING

Northbrook, IL

To anyone whose feet have ever stopped moving

To all those experiencing grief, anxiety, or
who are simply feeling lost

And to my daughter Zoey, who can finally understand me
and my dad jokes

www.masadapublishing.com | hello@masadapublishing.com

ISBN: 979-8-218-03922-6 (paperback)
ISBN: 979-8-218-03922-3 (ebook)

Cover photography by Cassandra Eldridge Miers

Ordering Information:
Special discounts are available on quantity purchases by corporations, associations, and others. For details, contact hello@keepthosefeetmoving.com or visit www. keepthosefeetmoving.com.

Publisher's Cataloging-in-Publication Data
Names: Coleman, A.J. (Alan J.), 1975-.
Title: Keep those feet moving : a widower's 8-step guide to coping with grief and
    thriving against all odds / A.J. Coleman.
Description: Northbrook, IL : Masada Publishing, 2023.
Identifiers: ISBN 9798218039226 (pbk.) | ISBN 9798218039223 (ebook)
Subjects: LCSH: Coleman, A.J. (Alan J.), 1975-. | Coleman, Cory M., 1977-2009. |
    Coleman, Zoey, 2008-. | Widowers – Life skills guides. | Bereavement – Religious
    aspects. | Grief. | Single fathers – United States. | Jerusalem. | Masada Site (Israel).
    | BISAC: BIOGRAPHY & AUTOBIOGRAPHY / Personal Memoirs. | SELF-HELP / Death,
    Grief, Bereavement. | FAMILY & RELATIONSHIPS / Parenting / Single Parent.
Classification: LCC HQ1058.C65 2023 | DDC 306.88 C—dc23

TABLE OF CONTENTS

KEEP THOSE FEET MOVING

A WIDOWER'S 8-STEP GUIDE TO COPING WITH GRIEF AND THRIVING AGAINST ALL ODDS

AJ COLEMAN

LETTER TO THE READER

Many of us don't know or understand what our life's purpose is or how to achieve it. And that's okay. I didn't know my life's purpose for a long time. Sometimes it takes an unthinkable event to occur in order for the purpose to reveal itself.

For me, it all began with a cancer diagnosis. No, not mine, it was my wife's diagnosis—brain cancer, with a prognosis of less than two years to live. From that moment on, my entire perception of life changed. The world looked different. I cried for a few moments and then collected my thoughts. I decided that no matter what was coming, I would rise up and fight alongside my wife.

It was during my wife's fight, and then ultimately when I lost her, that I discovered my life's mission: to inspire those directly or indirectly affected by cancer and other personal challenges to keep moving forward. However, to be completely honest, it took me some time to figure things out. In fact, it was a full five years after my wife's initial diagnosis before I finally broke my silence through blogging—I haven't looked back since.

The idea behind the title *Keep Those Feet Moving* was one of those random phrases that popped into my head one day. I'd been struggling to come up with exactly the right title for my blog for months. Nothing seemed to stick. I remember that it was a Saturday morning in late fall, and I had just picked up my shirts from the cleaners. At the stoplight, I ordinarily would turn right to proceed home. However, prior to turning, I noticed a long freight train slowly passing through the center of town and a logjam of cars waiting for the train to pass. Instead of waiting to turn right, I decided to turn left and take a different route home. It was longer, but at least I was in control, not the train. I muttered to myself, "Sometimes you gotta just keep those feet moving." Instantly, *Keep Those Feet Moving* was born!

Blogging provided some sense of personal achievement, but something was missing. I needed something bigger, a deeper way to connect with readers and myself. What I needed was to write a book so that I could use my story to inspire a greater number of people. But what did I know about writing a book? Absolutely nothing! I thought I could just copy and paste years of blog posts and—voilà. I was wrong. It turned out to be a much greater challenge than I expected. Those days of writing papers in high school and college did little to prepare me for writing an entire book. Luckily, I had a valued mentor and a team of book experts to guide me.

Defining my life's purpose has been a very useful footstep for me in finding comfort after the loss of my wife. It gave me something to strive for, which was to inspire and motivate others. Most of all, it provided personal guidance to better understand who I am and what I can do. I've learned that the setbacks, heartaches, and challenges in my life do not have to mean doom and gloom. Instead, they are meant to prepare me for the next steps in my life, while I continue to *keep those feet moving*.

Here's to the footsteps ahead!

AJ

FIND THE THRILL OF LIFE'S ROLLER COASTER

I like to think that life is like riding a roller coaster. You see, everyone rides roller coasters differently. Some scream or wave their hands in the air, while others sit without emotion. But regardless of how you ride, in the end everyone winds up in the same place. The true difference is in how you perceive the ride—was it terrifying or exhilarating? The same concept applies to how you perceive life.

My Footsteps

Back when I was in grade school, I once had an assignment to write my own obituary. Kind of creepy, right? If you've had a similar assignment, you may remember how difficult it was to write, both in terms of the context and the emotions involved.

The assignment required me to answer "Who am I?" and "How do I want to be remembered?" This happened so long ago, I don't even remember what I wrote. But I can definitely say that I never imagined my life would take the path it did. If only I'd known then what I know now.

Let's rewind for a moment to bring you up to speed. As a toddler, I was diagnosed with a hearing impairment. By the age of 20, I suffered from anxiety and panic attacks. At the age of 33, I became a widower and single father to a baby daughter. And, oh, throughout the years, I lost my job not once or twice but five separate times due to company layoffs or culture toxicity. At one point, I had less than $100 in my bank account and wasn't sure if I'd make the next rent payment or where my next meal was coming from.

From an early age, I'd grown quite accustomed to the fact that life knows no boundaries. There is no mercy button to push on the roller coaster when life is brutal and unfair. Life doesn't recognize how much you may be beaten down physically or emotionally. Life doesn't feel pain or have sympathy. It just keeps coming at you full speed each day. And when nightfall settles in, it doesn't go away; it's there waiting for you the next day.

What if I could rewrite the past? Go back in time to relive precious moments? Change the trajectory of my personal roller coaster ride? What if I hadn't been hearing impaired or a widower? What kind of life would I be leading? Would I be the same person I am today?

Let me rephrase all those questions as one: knowing what I know now, would I rewrite my life's script, starting years ago and changing the trajectory of my personal roller coaster ride?

The truth is, no matter what I could say or do, there are no what-ifs in life. There aren't any do-over buttons to push either.

My life's script was written as it was supposed to be written—from the moment I was born to the present moment. The script is part of the legacy I will one day leave behind: the ups, the downs, and everything in between. The past is now closed. It's best to accept it, learn from it, and move on. I suppose you can try to rewrite history as a way of finding personal comfort around troubling moments in your past. But when you alter life's script, it forever changes life's trajectory.

I use the term "life's script" as a way of describing what we start out with on our life's journey. I believe that from the moment we're born to the moment we ascend to the heavens, our life's script is already partially written. But along that journey, we come to various stopping points, forks in the road that can be life altering, thus influencing our life's script.

Deciding which path to follow at those stopping points depends on your primary instincts, logic, reasoning, and previous experiences. Perhaps guidance from trusted sources will assist you as well. Some people make those decisions easily, while others have no sense of direction and remain stuck in one place. But how do you know whether you made the right choice and selected the best path? The long answer is that sometimes you don't know and that only time will tell. The short answer is to trust your instincts and follow your heart.

Confused? Let me share another way to look at it. As a child, do you remember reading those "pick a path" stories where, when you get to the end of a chapter, you have to decide where the character should go next based on two or three options presented? If you choose option one, you are told to jump to a particular page. Choose another option, and you jump to another page. And when you come to the end of that particular chapter's script, you are again presented with more options to choose from. Each option has its own subset of stories based on the life's script chosen. By the end of the book, the character's life was entirely based on decisions made, which in turn affected the overall script.

My life changes daily, often instantaneously. Challenges I thought were resolved one day become unresolved the next. Trying to find a balance is like a game of roulette. I don't know what number or which color the ball will land on. I can strategically place my chips based on chance or statistics, and I can game-plan for what I want to accomplish, but fate ultimately controls the outcome. But what if there is a way that I can control the final outcome, change the odds, or perhaps change my overall legacy? What if I can take an unfavorable situation and turn it into a favorable one? Now I'm talking about an entirely different game altogether.

Many people have asked me where I get my strength. Much of it lies deep within me as I made a commitment to myself to rise higher with each setback, heartache, and challenge I've endured over the years. I taught myself early on not to accept defeat, not to accept failure. Those terms are not welcome in my vocabulary. With each challenge, I work hard to overcome it, preparing myself for the next one to surface. I always *keep those feet moving,* never stopping to rest. If I can't knock down walls, I find ways around them. If I can't find a way around, I make my own way. I made a decision a long time ago to decide what I choose to accept and what I don't.

I've had my world rocked on more than a few occasions. I've been knocked down emotionally and mentally so many times that I've lost count, but I will tell you, I don't count how many times I've been knocked down—I count how many times I rise back up.

You'll never see me struggle. You'll never see me give up. Why? Because I've taught myself to believe that I am too strong, too determined to succumb to defeat and pressure. I've trained myself to exceed expectations, to overcome challenges. It's my perception that enables me to believe in myself.

Every morning when I wake up, I remind myself how blessed I am for the new day. Although I might not understand the "why" or might not like all the twists and turns from the day before, I know I've been given another chance to *keep those feet moving.* Throughout the day, no matter what battles I've faced, all I need to do is just make it through one inch at a time, one step at a time. And if I can do that, I can change the trajectory of the roller coaster. When I lie down to sleep every evening, I always remember to say thank you for the opportunities given to me that day, knowing that tomorrow will repeat—presenting new challenges—and I'll need to be ready.

Each of us carries little secrets that help drive us toward our successes in life, especially when the roller coaster suddenly speeds downward. My secrets aren't anything out of the ordinary—no superpowers or time travel involved. I draw conclusions based on logic and reasoning, or I look to philosophical words of wisdom. I know I can't meet every challenge alone—sometimes I need to draw strength from outside in the form of inspirational poems.

Here are my two favorite poems that I recite to myself each morning to empower me to take on life's challenges. Both are very personal for me, and I cherish the meanings behind them. Even during my darkest moments, I draw motivation and comfort from these words, knowing that they help guide me.

"The Guy in the Glass"
—Dale Wimbrow, 1934

When you get what you want in your struggle for pelf,

And the world makes you King for a day,

Then go to the mirror and look at yourself,

And see what that guy has to say.

For it isn't your Father, or Mother, or Wife,

Who judgment upon you must pass.

The feller whose verdict counts most in your life

Is the guy staring back from the glass.

He's the feller to please, never mind all the rest,

For he's with you clear up to the end,

And you've passed your most dangerous, difficult test

If the guy in the glass is your friend.

You may be like Jack Horner and "chisel" a plum,

And think you're a wonderful guy,

But the man in the glass says you're only a bum

If you can't look him straight in the eye.

You can fool the whole world down the pathway of years,

And get pats on the back as you pass,

But your final reward will be heartaches and tears

If you've cheated the guy in the glass.[1]

Pledge of Success
—Unknown

Today is a new day, a new beginning.

It has been given to me as a new gift.

I can either use it or throw it away.

What I do today will affect me tomorrow.

I cannot blame anyone but myself if I do not succeed.

I promise to use this day to the fullest by giving my best, realizing it can never come back again.

This is my life and I choose to make it a success!

Roller coasters are designed to bring excitement, joy, and thrills—just as life is meant to. Every moment counts in this precious life. Every day counts. While it's easy to be discouraged and disenchanted when you face each challenge, remember that you can always turn it around—find the silver lining, and turn it around. That brings me back to the school assignment I told you about, when I was required to answer the question "How do I want to be remembered?" Here's what I'd write today:

I want to be remembered as someone who took personal hardships and fought through each and every one of them. Each

---

1   Dale Wimbrow, "The Guy in the Glass," The Guy in the Glass, accessed April 26, 2022, https://www.theguyintheglass.com/gig.htm.

time I got knocked down, I rose back up stronger.

I want to be remembered as someone who inspired others to prove there's a lot of good left in this world. Someone who performed selfless acts of kindness without asking for any return. Someone who served as a reminder that there are angels and saints walking among us.

I want to be remembered as someone who knows he was blessed for all that he has, not for what he's lost. Someone who fully appreciated the opportunities given to him over the years, knowing he made the very best of them.

I want to be remembered as someone who spent life giving back to others. Someone who provided support to those who needed it most. Someone who helped others rise back onto their feet by giving them the strength and courage to do so.

I want to be remembered as a loving father to my daughter each day. That, despite the loss of her mother, I did my best to give her both what a father and a mother provide. I may not have had true "motherly" instincts, but I continued to let her know how much she was loved by me and many others.

Life isn't always perfect. But every once in a while, a pleasant surprise is presented in a way that makes a profound impact. That pleasant surprise could be anything that touches you in a positive way. It might be as short term as a ray of sunshine on your face that brightens your day. Or it could be long term, such as hearing there is a cure for a medical condition you've been experiencing or finding out about a financial windfall.

When all is said and done, each pleasant surprise will enable you to take a step forward to *keep those feet moving*.

Your Footsteps

I love to use analogies to describe certain situations or moments. It helps put things into perspective, perhaps making them more relatable. That is why the roller coaster analogy is the perfect starting point for putting life into perspective.

Every day you ride your own roller coaster. You go up and down, twisting and turning. There are high speed drops that make you question if you can stand up to the challenges. If you talk to one person, the ride might be their worst nightmare; others may be completely indifferent to it.

When things aren't going your way, how often do you start looking for that downward slope? Waiting for the next terrible moment to strike? As the series of events mounts and swells, you probably ask yourself negative questions: "Why does this always happen to me?" "What are the odds?" "Will my luck ever change?" "Really, did that just happen?"

But what if I told you that the next turn doesn't always have to trend downward? Instead of looking down, look up. Look ahead and keep looking up. Reach out to touch the sky. Imagine what it'll feel like in your outstretched arms. Look around to appreciate the surrounding views. Feel your body become weightless, free from all the strife in your life. Feel your heart skip with excitement, and sense the thrill of triumph as you ascend to the top. Sit mighty in your seat and enjoy this moment, for you are about to take control by changing a negative moment and making it positive!

When you change your perception of your surroundings, you gain control of the situation. Suddenly, the challenge at hand may not be such a challenge after all.

Remember, your perceptions are a reflection of your true emotional and cognitive state. Your position at the precise moment when a challenge or setback arises will dictate your approach and, eventually, the outcome. Certainly, there are those who spend their entire lives searching for a way to exit the roller coaster because the ride is either too scary or too painful to endure. But what's fascinating is that, when you're on an actual roller coaster, it's the upward climb that drives the anticipation and the downward drop that provides the thrill. In life, it's the exact opposite—you want to stay on the upward climb indefinitely.

I'll admit, when certain types of challenges arise, it's nearly impossible to change your mindset. The loss of a loved one, a physical injury, the loss of a job, and financial constraints can quickly lead to a downward spiral. In those instances, the emotional pain may be too great to mend quickly. Emotions dictate your thoughts and actions, resulting in a fast downward slide. You are consumed by the anxiety that surrounds the challenge itself. You ultimately feel lost, not knowing where to go next. So, what *do* you do?

You need to find a balance somewhere to slowly level the playing field. The sooner you find your balance and sit mighty on the roller coaster, the sooner you'll feel in control again.

Here's the reality: What's happened has already happened, and it can't be changed. You can't go backward to avert it or stay fixated on it in disgust. Instead, what you *can* do is to find the strength within you to move forward and not look back—not even a slight turn of the head. Just keep looking ahead. No one said it would be easy. It'll take serious effort and determination to push through the barriers. But baby steps are all you need. It isn't a race. You have to learn to walk before you can run.

Although history has been written, the future has not. Some believe the past defines the future or that statistics will dictate a pending outcome. It's debatable. As a whole, we spend so much time thinking about the past and playing hypothetical what-if games, we neglect to establish our own boundaries for what we choose to accept in life. Even during our greatest challenges, we catch ourselves looking into the rearview mirror. Understandably, you may not be able to control every aspect of your life, but you can learn to channel your mindset to thinking logically instead of emotionally.

The next time you're on a roller coaster, stop and think about your perceptions of the experience. Is it really a downward slope, or are you just looking at it with a slightly different perspective that makes it *feel* like a downward slope?

Our Footsteps

Without question, the most difficult step in what I like to call "creating motion" is simply getting started. It can be helpful to have a blueprint, a set of instructions, or—in *Keep Those Feet Moving* terms—to follow the trail that will lead you to the right path. I know from experience that my steps for creating motion work and that you can apply them and make them work for your life too. Although I can't pretend to always have the answers or fully explain why certain things happen in life, I know I have a different mentality than most in the way I approach and interpret things. While research and articles found on the internet may provide educational or expert guidance, I prefer to use logic, reasoning, and philosophical approaches.

Below are my five steps to help *keep those feet moving* to better ride life's roller coaster.

1. SEIZE THE DAY.

Make no mistake, life is precious. Each day is a gift, and it's up to you to make the best of what you've been given. If you don't like where you currently stand, then get moving! It doesn't matter how or where you're headed, as long as you're moving. Motion creates action! Circle around and try different approaches. If one door doesn't open, try the next and the next. Keep trying until a door opens. Even if it does open, it may not offer the best approach, so don't settle. Don't shy away from obstacles. Embrace them as building blocks. You can't give up, no matter what the challenges are. Find a way to push yourself to *keep those feet moving*. Every day is an opportunity to make a difference for yourself but only if you seize it.

2. GIVE YOURSELF AN HONEST ASSESSMENT.

If you find yourself run down with low energy and you're confused about how to change the course of action ahead, take a look at yourself in the mirror. Give yourself an honest assessment of where you are emotionally and mentally without any hesitation or doubts. Your first instinct is typically the honest one. Remember that if you don't like your initial reaction, you have the power to change your perspective, which in turn can change your roller coaster ride's trajectory.

3. ASK YOURSELF, "WHO AM I?"

Who you are and what you are represent two different things, although they are often mistakenly interchanged. Your career, hobbies, and passions are *what* you are. But it's *who* you are that defines your legacy and how you're remembered. What do you want others to say about you? That's *who* you are. It's a subtle yet meaningful difference.

Many different negative labels have been used to describe me: impaired, widower, or single father. But although those labels represent certain aspects of my life, they are not who I am!

4. Ask yourself, "Have you truly done all that you can do?"

Every day, ask yourself whether you've truly done all you can do. If at any point negative phrases like "I can't" or "I tried but" become part of your routine vocabulary, then the answer is simple. You haven't done everything you can do. You haven't given it your best effort. Instead, you're merely looking for an easy way out that doesn't exist. Sure it's easier giving up and walking away from a battle, but giving up results in heartache and pain. And although giving up might be a common way out for many, it doesn't have to be for you. You are stronger than that. Tell yourself that there are no more excuses. You know what you have to do. Earn the respect you deserve. No matter how many times you get knocked down, get back up and try again and again.

5. Believe in yourself.

Never stop believing. As long as you continue to fight, you're doing everything you can. Medical science doesn't define you; you define medical science. Misfortunes don't limit you; you can rise above them. Fate doesn't control your destiny; you control your destiny. Every day, battles come and go—that's a part of life. But only you can decide how you want to fight, and you can only fight successfully if you believe in yourself.

Self-Reflection Footsteps

Defining life's purpose should be engaging and fun as you discover a lot about yourself and your goals. While "Our Footsteps" provided starter steps, the following are key summary points, self-guided questions, and self-reflection exercises to help you find the thrill of life's roller coaster ride.

KEY SUMMARY POINTS

1. Change your perception of life to change your life's roller coaster trajectory.

2. When it comes to your past, sometimes it's better to accept it and move on.

3. Although your past may be written, your future is not—now is your opportunity to go and get what you want.

SELF-GUIDED QUESTIONS

1. What are your life's goals? What do you want to achieve short term vs. long term?

____

____

____

2. Ask yourself and then define "Who are you?"

____

____

____

3. How do you want to be remembered? What will others say about you?

____

____

____

____

SELF-REFLECTION EXERCISES

1. Find your roller coaster thrill.

Not all roller coaster rides are filled with downward slopes followed by twists and turns. What if you could design your own life's roller coaster? What would that look like? Take a piece of paper and sketch it out. Pay careful attention to the peaks and valleys, twists and turns. Do you have too many? Not enough? How high will you project the upward climb? Have fun with your design. See if you can model it to your current life, or if you are that creative, perhaps you can change the trajectory!

2. Create your own success story.

You're often inspired and motivated by the achievements of others, so why not create your own success story? Make it a story that is so inspirational that it can be used as a springboard to motivate others or, just as importantly, to achieve success yourself. Don't forget to share it, because others are going to want to read your story!

3. Impose a 60-day challenge on yourself.

Self-imposed challenges are an opportunity to make changes for the better. For example, if you need to refocus on mental health, rebuild a relationship, or earn more money, it's amazing what you can accomplish in just 60 days. Only by challenging yourself can you achieve more personal satisfaction as you reach new heights in life. Write down your action plan, and post it where you can review it daily to marvel at your accomplishments.

Too often, we accept what's been given to us as part of our life's script. Reluctant to challenge unfavorable outcomes such as medical diagnoses, grief, and job losses, we instead tend to exhibit passive behaviors and struggle to move forward.

You could create the argument that much of it is out of our control and that nothing can be done about it. But I challenge you to think otherwise. There are *always* options. It's up to you to decide whether you want to act upon those options. In any situation, there are two outcomes: favorable or unfavorable. No gray areas, simply straight forward.

By sharing these personal experiences, I hope you will see that I am just like you, but I believe that every challenge has its own solution. It's a matter of first recognizing the obstacles, then creating a response. If I had listened every time someone told me I couldn't do something or told me no, I wouldn't have been able to write this book you're reading today, nor would I have been able to *keep those feet moving*.

2

TRANSFORM DISABILITY AND CHALLENGES INTO ABILITY AND OPPORTUNITIES

Each one of us possesses a special gift that makes us unique. Some of us are outspoken and become advocates; others prefer to keep their thoughts to themselves. It's a matter of personal preference. No one should be judged or ridiculed either way. Society as a whole can be critical or accepting depending on personal values, pressures, and experiences. In the end, there are always life lessons to be shared and learned.

My Footsteps

It was supposed to be a routine visit to the pediatrician's office for what my parents thought was another ear infection. The year was 1979, and I was three years old. By that time my parents had grown rather accustomed to these types of doctor's office visits.

Most young kids battle common colds and viruses. I got lots of ear infections.

But this particular office visit was different. The pediatrician noticed something during the examination and immediately referred us to an audiologist for a hearing test. After a series of painstaking and frightening tests (especially for a three-year-old), I was diagnosed with a mild to severe hearing impairment in both ears. The diagnosis was a relief in the sense that it answered my parents' many lingering concerns. Apparently, there were times when I confused my own name with "yeah," because when I called out to my mother, she would respond, "Yeah?" Other times, I wouldn't answer when people spoke to me, because I couldn't hear them.

Shortly after the diagnosis, my parents wondered whether my hearing impairment was caused by my numerous ear infections or if I'd been born with the impairment. It wasn't until many years later that I learned that the tiny inner ear hair cells, which move sound through the ear, didn't develop properly when I was in my mother's womb.

Today, according to the National Institute on Deafness and Other Communication Disorders, "about 2 to 3 out of every 1,000 children in the United States are born with a detectable level of hearing loss in one or both ears."[2]

To compensate for my hearing impairment, I was outfitted with what seemed to be the world's largest hearing aids. Okay, maybe not the world's largest, but huge. Back then, in the '70s, hearing aid technology wasn't as advanced as it is today. Hearing

---

2 "Quick Statistics About Hearing," National Institute on Deafness and Other Communication Disorders, last modified March 25, 2021, https://www.nidcd.nih.gov/health/statistics/quick-statistics-hearing.

aids now are tiny and far more powerful than they were back then when the processor or amplifier was rather clunky and protruded from behind the ear. Manufacturers then didn't make the kinds of hearing aids that are placed directly in the ear canal as you often see today.

As a preschooler, I was unaware of and unprepared for what struggles lay ahead. All I knew at the time was that I needed hearing aids to hear sounds, speak clearly, and perhaps actually listen to instructions or scolding.

Compared to many other disabilities or health-related issues, I'm sure the general public would agree that a hearing impairment is considered immaterial or a "micro concern." But try telling that to a young child or a teenager who just wants to blend in. As a result, for as long as I can remember, I've always seemed to be in my own world. I compensated for what I couldn't hear by reading lips, anticipating next moves, and trying to outsmart everyone else. I lived a very private life. In some ways it was as if I lived a double life—not the secret agent type, but one that hides behind an impairment or disability. Unless you knew me as a child, you'd never know about my disability. Why is that?

Growing up with a disability in the '70s and '80s was very different than it is today. There were far fewer resources available to educate parents, and other kids were far less accepting of classmates with disabilities. There were no social platforms that one could turn to for support. My parents did the best they could to shelter me, but in the end, neither they nor I was fully educated about my disability and the challenges I would face both physically and mentally.

My first exposure to the social challenges of having a hearing impairment came in kindergarten. There was a specialized program at the elementary school dedicated to educating deaf children. That may sound like a good thing, but I was not enrolled in the specialized program. I was enrolled in kindergarten without any specific accommodations. However, just a few days into the school year, my classmates poked fun at me and the other deaf students because we couldn't hear them. Some of the cruelest classmates mocked me into believing there was something physically wrong with me and that I was not perceived as "normal." To them, there was no difference between deaf and hearing impaired.

From that day forward, I was scarred. The jeers were horrifying. They were social cruelty in its worst form and led to a harsh realization for me as to how society looks down on those who are different. It was those moments at such a young and impressionable age that cemented the foundation for my future insecurities.

From that first humiliating day in kindergarten to today, I did all I could to protect myself from harm and those jeers. I overworked myself to prove my value and, ultimately, lived that double life because I would rather hide the truth than risk being bullied or left feeling insecure.

As I grew into my teenage years, those very scars grew too. Classmates from grade school to high school continued to bully me, poking fun at whether I could hear them, or mockingly repeating, "What?" in an effort to tease. Why? Because I was still perceived differently. No one else in the school had a hearing aid. That was how I was known and labeled.

Through those years, I developed a fear that if people knew about my hearing impairment, I would be subject to ridicule, which would lead to not having as many friendships or career and romantic opportunities as those with normal hearing. Rather than get the professional help I needed to better understand my hearing impairment and learn how to embrace it, I fought a lonely battle within myself as I placed social acceptance on a pedestal above everything in life.

College was the best time of my life. At the University of Florida, the chance to start over again was extremely liberating, because no one there knew about my past or my hearing impairment. Although I knew I would struggle to hear in class and in certain social settings, I removed my hearing aids immediately and went to work building my social image.

Armed with new confidence and goals, it felt as if I was one of the most popular guys on campus. Guys in the fraternity house greeted me with high fives and handshakes. Girls greeted me with hugs and kisses. It was like paradise, a dream that I never wanted to see end—a complete 180-degree turnaround from the torment of middle school and high school.

But all of that came with a price. Despite the popularity and enjoyment of life's pleasures, deep down I felt as if I was deceiving everyone. I often wondered, "If people knew about my hearing impairment, would they still treat me the same? Would I still be 'one of the guys' or have the same types of friendships? Would I still have the time of my life in college?"

Perhaps, but I'll never know, because I never spoke a word about it to anyone. In the end, being socially accepted was more important to me and worth the sacrifice of not hearing properly.

After I graduated from the University of Florida in 1998 with a bachelor of science degree in advertising and a minor in business administration, I moved out west to obtain my MBA from the University of Arizona. Graduate school proved to be a very different experience than college had been, partly because I was one of the youngest students in the MBA program but also because my goals were vastly different. College was about enjoying the greatest time of my life; graduate school was about studies and career preparation. For a split second, I thought about bringing out those hearing aids and actually wearing them. It was time: My college chapter was closed, and it was now time to get serious. It was time to move on from the past and reprioritize my social image. But as soon as I sat down for orientation and introductions began, I reverted.

For my entire time in college and graduate school and during my career, I sacrificed the ability to hear for social acceptance: I was too ashamed of my hearing impairment, too scared to open up. Oh, wait, there was a time when I actually wore my hearing aids to work for the first few days of a new job in 2013. It was a prestigious analytical position within a corporation. There was just one issue—the environment was filled with white noise. If you aren't familiar with white noise, it generates sounds over a wide range of frequencies, masking various noise interruptions, which in turn draws out added noise. To an individual with a hearing impairment, white noise makes it even more difficult to hear. Unfortunately, the hearing aids I had did not counter the effects of white noise.

Due to the white noise impact, I still needed hearing aids to help me hear properly. On the third day of the job, my manager was sitting next me training me on a particular task and made a remark that still echoes to this day. She stated, "I didn't know you wear hearing aids."

As soon as she said that, I panicked. I froze. I fought back tears. If she had known during the hiring process, would I have been hired? What would this mean for future promotions at the company? Would a comment be entered in my HR profile? Was the fact that I didn't check the box stating that I have a disability on the employment application grounds for termination?

So many millions of thoughts ran through my head—one small comment and my entire past and fears circled back. The next day, upon arrival at work, I removed my hearing aids— again. Perhaps I could have filed a complaint or a concern report with HR, as I knew laws were in place to protect those with disabilities. But by then, I was too afraid of losing my job, as I needed a salary to support myself and my daughter.

My hearing impairment is part of my personal roller coaster, filled with twists and turns and followed by peaks and valleys. As I continue to ride along today, it's easy to see that instead of facing my fears and understanding my hearing impairment back then, I was merely masking them, thinking that one day everything would suddenly be okay. As it turns out, that one day is today.

You see, in all those years, I never realized I had a superhero power that I used daily in every type of scenario. I'm not sure how I acquired it. Perhaps I was born with it or simply perfected it over the years.

We think of superhero powers as belonging to characters in Marvel movies or video games, or to those who like to re-enact their childhood fantasies. People like you and me don't really think of any talents we might have as superpowers. But we have them! I like to call them "special gifts."

For a hearing-impaired individual, lip reading is the ultimate power. Being able to decipher and anticipate dialogue quickly, then filling in the gaps between words provides an unmatched strength. It's the key to success. Although others may take it for granted, lip reading is a survival skill or, truly, a superpower!

I may not always hear you or decipher each word exactly, but I watch your lips and eyes closely. I may take an extended pause to comprehend what I hear and what I think you said before responding. And do I always get it right? No. I may only get part of what you said or, worse, completely miss the beginning of what you said and decipher the entire conversation incorrectly. That, in turn, triggers a response that's not consistent with the conversation or creates a bit of embarrassment.

I've never spoken the phrase "I can't hear you" publicly. Out of embarrassment and forcibly trying to mitigate my impairment, I was always quick to pick up on my impairment mistakes based on reactions, confusion, or occasional sneers.

Lip reading requires one essential: I need to see your lips move. Whether you are two feet away or 20, your lips are what I focus on most when you speak. For a hearing-impaired individual, sight serves as the primary sensory organ, as the eyes can quickly diffuse any situation by logic and reasoning. So, in a sense, the COVID-19 pandemic became my kryptonite: As long as a mask is worn, I feel powerless. The old way of navigating through was forever changed.

Throughout the pandemic, I've learned that there are more important things in life than fighting to keep my hearing impairment concealed. I often think about the people who lost their lives or those fighting to live one more day. How many of them would gladly trade testing positive for COVID-19 for a hearing impairment? Compared to life's *big* problems, a hearing impairment might be truly considered small potatoes.

It wasn't until I sat down to write this book that I realized something had to change. How could I be an inspiration to others if I didn't come clean about who I am, what my struggles are, and how I overcame my own insecurities? That is why I decided to share how I transitioned my disability into ability and no longer allow my hearing impairment to define me.

One of the many life lessons I've learned is that it isn't about where you start—it's where you finish that matters most. Setbacks lead to comebacks, and the experience as a whole leads to invaluable teaching moments. I was born with a hearing impairment; without it I would not be who I am today.

Oh, and guess what—I now wear a hearing aid every day! Pretty cool, isn't it?

Your Footsteps

According to the Centers of Disease Control and Prevention (CDC), disability is defined as "any condition of the body or mind (impairment) that makes it more difficult for the person with the condition to do certain activities (activity limitation) and interact with the world around them (participation restrictions)."[3] There are many types of disabilities, such as those that affect a person's

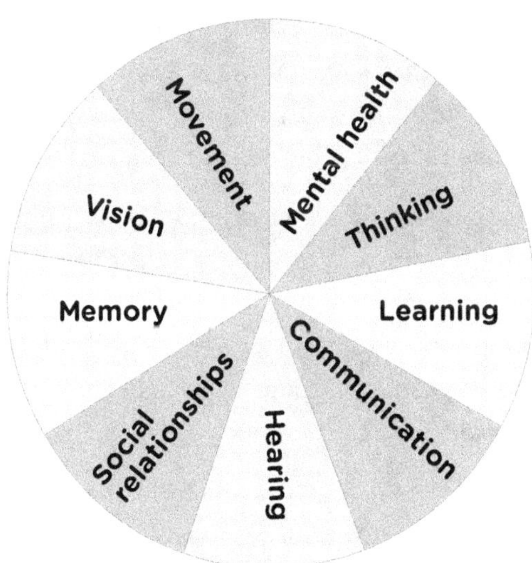

---

3 "Impairments, Activity Limitations, and Participation Restrictions," Centers for Disease Control and Prevention, last modified September 16, 2020, https://www.cdc.gov/ncbddd/disabilityandhealth/disability.html.

There are many books and websites available to research the definition of "disability"; however, I find the CDC's explanation the best, making it not only understandable but relatable. If you read further on their website, you will obtain a deeper understanding of the definition and how the CDC actually distinguishes the difference between disability and impairment.

Whether you were born with a disability, became disabled, or know someone with a disability directly or indirectly, there are a certain number of physical, emotional, and mental elements to consider. Much of it starts with the perception of how you feel about the disability and the personal impacts it has on your life. Values, personalities, experiences, and support are all contributing factors to your perception. The good news is that perceptions can often change with a proper education and understanding.

Returning to the CDC website, "although 'people with disabilities' sometimes refers to a single population, this is actually a diverse group of people with a wide range of needs. Two people with the same type of disability can be affected in very different ways. Some disabilities may be hidden or not easy to see."[4]

To be honest, I feel this description is on point with my experience. Although my hearing impairment negatively affected me, another person may have a different, more positive experience. That's the beauty of perception and why no disability is exactly alike for any two people. The same notion goes back to how we all ride roller coasters differently, as discussed in chapter 1.

While it's important to touch on each disability, I'd like to pivot a bit in another direction to provide more inspiration and motivation to those directly or indirectly affected.

---

4 "Impairments, Activity Limitations, and Participation Restrictions," Centers for Disease Control and Prevention.

In general, you set goals in life and standards you abide by. Your perceptions dictate whether or not you succeed. Strength comes from within, and toughness becomes an important attribute. Too often, toughness is thought of as a physical attribute. In reality, it's more mental. Once you get into a zone, it's not the physical aspect that propels you; it's the motivation, focus, and commitment. Most fail not because they lack physical strength but the mental capacity to overcome.

Every individual needs some level of inspiration and motivation. Whether we're overcoming a short-term disability or one that's life changing, there must be an initial triggering or aha moment. Often, the first thing we do is search for alternatives that inspire, motivate, or fire us up. I like to call it "establishing your zone" as your zone becomes your center of balance, your rock. It sets the tone for what you will accept going forward in life.

Life does throw curves (a.k.a. challenges) that change the momentum. Ever notice just when everything seems to fall into place—career, relationships, finances, health—suddenly, without warning, the unexpected occurs? That's the curve. Although many consider curves negative attributes, perhaps they need to be looked at as forms of motivation. Without pain, there is no gain.

Shift your focus and concentrate on your goal. All realistic goals are attainable, so set your sights high. Each day, work toward your goal and climb a little higher. Filter out any white noise surrounding you, and maintain your focus on what you truly want to achieve in life. Keep your focus centered and stay true to your zone.

Commitment enables you to stay motivated and focused. Any obstacles you face along your journey are overshadowed by your determination. Your instincts will tell you when to push harder, move faster, and climb higher. Failure and quitting are not options—you've got to strive further and stay committed to your goals.

You will succeed. Erase any lingering doubts and other people's perceptions. None of those matter. The most important elements are you and your ability to overcome challenges despite the odds. You can go around in fear, holding onto sorrow or self-pity, or you can go around with your head held high, confident and determined. Support can provide guidance and help you stay in your zone, but ultimately, the choice is yours.

Fears erode your confidence level. They become a mental block and are very difficult to overcome in certain situations. Recently, I've come to the conclusion that when you develop a fear of overcoming your impairment or disability as I did, you then become limited and your ability to navigate through becomes much tougher. Sometimes I wonder whether it's really your own perceptions that create and elevate your fears.

If you go through life in fear, you'll never capitalize on opportunities. You'll be hindered in your potential and that will have a direct influence on the outcome. You can't go through life being afraid of something that may or may not happen. The more you focus on your fears and the potential mishaps ahead, the greater your risk of actually not succeeding.

You can hide behind fears, or you can conquer them, gain new confidence, gain new strength, and ascend to new heights. Don't let fear define you. Instead, you define fear. Never back down and never hide. For every punch you are hit with, fight back. Look at your impairment or disability challenges directly and regain control. This is about you. This is your life; live how you want to live. Fear is not welcome anymore.

There was a song written in the early '80s, "Eye of the Tiger" by Survivor. I am sure you've heard of it, but if you haven't, I encourage you to stop reading right now and go listen to it or Google the lyrics—they're about rising to the challenge. Take a deep breath and exhale one more time. This is where motivation is drawn from. Feel the power of the lyrics.

Everywhere there is opportunity to be inspired and uplifted. It doesn't always come to you. Sometimes you have to go search for it, and make it happen. Or, in the worst case, create it on your own. Life is full of challenges. When you add disability challenges to life's equation, it becomes a bit more complicated, but it doesn't have to be. In the end, it all comes down to perception and finding balance. Why not change life's equation to make it work for you? Remove the term "disability challenges," and replace it with "ability challenges." Now take a look at life's equation. Much, much better!

Our Footsteps

Thirty years ago, there were limited resources and technology available to those with disabilities, including hearing impairments. Fortunately, there have been many advancements in medical science and technology. As a society, children and adults are now better educated about social acceptance of those with disabilities.

Through research and self-reflection, I've created four steps called iCAN for helping others overcome disabilities, impairments, or other challenges in general. These steps are impact, compensate, accept, and naturally inspire.

1. IMPACT

Learn everything you can about the disability diagnosis and its impact on quality of life. Whether the disability affects you directly or indirectly, ask many questions and seek multiple opinions if necessary. Understand that the emotional responses you're feeling are normal and that you're not alone. Never compare yourself to others, as the story is not yet finalized. There is an open script that still needs to be written.

2. COMPENSATE

You can compensate for your disability challenges by defying the odds, knocking down barriers, and pushing further and harder than the others. Create your own story, and make the impossible become possible. And remember to always celebrate your accomplishments no matter how immaterial they may seem at the time.

3. ACCEPT

Accept and embrace who you are. Stay positive and don't channel your energy toward negatives or unknowns. Never give up hope, because medical science and technology are producing miracles each day. Smile, because your disability doesn't define you; it's how you *accept* it that does.

4. NATURALLY INSPIRE

Become an advocate and naturally inspire others by sharing your story. Helping others is a tremendously rewarding healing mechanism. Create a movement (or a blog) that increases awareness about your disability. Define your legacy footprint, something you'll leave behind to inspire and motivate others.

The beauty of iCAN is that you can use the same concepts and expand upon them to transition any disability to ability. Although society as a whole may attempt to define you, ultimately, I believe you have the ability to define society by the way you can use *your* influence to overcome the general term "disability."

In conjunction with the iCAN steps, I'd like to share the impacts of COVID-19 on hearing-impaired individuals. Despite not being able to read lips through masks, I've learned to compensate through these three alternative steps.

1. USE AN INTERPRETER AS A BUFFER.

Usually reserved for foreign language speakers or for live public service announcements, interpreters can easily serve as a buffer between those wearing a mask and yourself. Find a family member or friend you trust to accompany you to places where you may need assistance with interpretation. Not only will an interpreter relieve you from the burden of those embarrassing and frustrating moments, but they will also provide you with company.

2. TRUST YOUR EYESIGHT AND ANTICIPATE THE UNEXPECTED.

Be vigilant and scan your surroundings to identify any unexpected traps or barriers. For the hearing impaired, that might mean situations where there is a lot of background noise, street noise, or white noise. Or sometimes it may be the inability to read lips due to the angle of the speaker, a substance blocking the view, or a mask being worn. It's always better to see ahead than to be surprised unexpectedly.

3. PLAN AHEAD AND STAY ON POINT.

The keys to running errands, shopping, and picking up take-out are to plan ahead and not deviate from the plan. Make lists and study store layouts prior to going there. Order ahead and arrange for precise pickups. In doing so, you'll minimize verbal interactions, which will make the outing more manageable. Any deviation from the plan could rattle self-confidence.

Forget about the CDC's recommendations and the public's divided opinions on vaccinations for a moment—one thing is certain: masks or no masks, there are many hearing-impaired individuals combating the pandemic from a different perspective.

Self-Reflection Footsteps

I've shared personal insights on transitioning from disability into ability, and below are key summary points, self-guided questions, and self-reflection exercises to consider.

KEY SUMMARY POINTS

1. Disabilities, impairments, and challenges don't define you—you define them.

2. Erase any lingering doubts and other people's perceptions. None of those matter.

3. Life will always throw you curves (challenges). How you respond will knock the curve out of the zone.

SELF-GUIDED QUESTIONS

1. What are your greatest fears? How and why have they become your fears?

____

____

____

____

2. What is your superhero power? How can you use it to overcome challenges?

____

____

____

____

3. How have you transformed challenges into opportunities? What steps did you take?

____

____

____

____

SELF-REFLECTION EXERCISES

1. **Think about your past encounters with someone with a disability challenge.**

Think back to a previous encounter with someone with a disability—it could be a hearing impairment, a physical condition, or an appearance issue. Did you attempt to accommodate them, or did you struggle to maintain composure by showing frustration? How could you have handled the encounter better? What would you have done differently? Sometimes taking a step backward to look at the situation from a different perspective helps you take a step forward to better understand the disability. Although you can't change the past, you can be empathetic in the future.

2. **Create your own iCAN concepts.**

Using the iCAN concept, take a sheet of paper and write down your own iCAN concepts as they relate to you personally. Or perhaps be creative and develop your own abbreviated step process. If you want to get really creative, construct a board game for others to join. By creating a board game, not only will you be able to see the concepts laid out, but you'll also be able to use the very same concepts to educate and inspire others to overcome their disability.

3. **Advocate on behalf of those with disabilities.**

How has this chapter provided you with a new perspective on those with disabilities? What can you do to help educate others who are directly or indirectly affected by disabilities? How can you become an advocate? Join an advocacy group, write an article to be shared with an editor for publication, or volunteer your time and services to those in need. Being an advocate is not only rewarding, but it also provides an opportunity to give back to an important cause.

In a sense, by opening up about my hearing impairment in this book, I've marked it as a true declaration of my long-awaited acceptance of who I am. It may have taken me 46 years to acknowledge, but I found the courage and strength to take the steps forward—not to mention that there's a part of me that now feels liberated from a burden I've carried my entire life. That chapter of my life is now closed as I continue to *keep those feet moving*.

FOOTSTEP

3

SPRING INTO MENTAL SELF-CARE

Often taken for granted, our mental health or mental well-being is an aspect of our lives that many neglect. Perhaps the term "mental" is perceived negatively or is associated with someone who has a mental disorder. Or maybe it's just easier to create an excuse rather than take the time to focus on well-being. Regardless, mental health should be a top priority and vital focal point of our lives.

What if the term is replaced with mental self-care, which can vastly improve your mental and physical health? It can play a consequential part that involves your psychological, emotional, and social well-being. In other words, it correlates to how you think, feel, act, or respond in certain situations, and it can influence how you handle stress, relate to others, and make choices. With that being said, why isn't there a greater emphasis on mental self-care? I think much of it relates to life's daily rigors, time commitments, and perhaps education.

My Footsteps

What do Ryan Reynolds, Ellie Goulding, Selena Gomez, Jennifer Lopez, Emma Stone, Adele, and Johnny Depp all have in common? Yes, they all are well-known celebrities who star in movies or perform on stage. But you may be surprised to learn that these celebrities we love and idolize all suffer from some form of anxiety or panic attacks!

What's fascinating is that if you remove the fame, the glitz, and the paparazzi, these celebrities are the same as you and me: just ordinary people affected by a mental health condition. Naturally, your first reaction is apt to be that you'd be glad to trade places anytime, but if you read deeper into their stories, you'll understand why and how their mental health conditions came about.

"I have anxiety, I've always had anxiety," Ryan Reynolds told the *New York Times* in May 2018.[5] "Both in the lighthearted 'I'm anxious about this' kind of thing, and I've been to the depths of the darker end of the spectrum, which is not fun."[6] The *Deadpool* actor says growing up with a tough father influenced him as a kid, and the effects may have followed him into adulthood. "He wasn't easy on anyone. And he wasn't easy on himself. I think the anxiety might have started there, trying to find ways to control others by trying to control myself."[7]

Jennifer Lopez had a panic attack during a photo shoot. "As I sat there getting made up, my heart was beating out of my chest,

---

5   Cara Buckley, "This Story Has Already Stressed Ryan Reynolds Out," New York Times, May 2, 2018, https://www.nytimes.com/2018/05/02/movies/ryan-reynolds-deadpool-2.html.

6   Buckley, "This Story."

7   Ramin Setoodeh, "How 'Deadpool' Saved Ryan Reynolds," *Variety*, January 3, 2017, https://variety.com/2017/film/features/ryan-reynolds-deadpool-golden-globes-1201951103/.

and I felt as if I couldn't breathe … I became consumed with anxiety," Lopez revealed in her memoir *True Love*.[8] At the time, she says she felt as if she was "going crazy."

Emma Stone revealed that she started dealing with anxiety at seven years old. "That's when I started having panic attacks, which I've talked about pretty extensively. I think your wiring is just kind of what you are. My mom always says that I was born with my nerves outside of my body," Stone said.[9] While opening up about it was scary for her, she says it has been "very healing," along with therapy and medication.[10] Stone emphasized: Anxiety "is something that is part of me, but it's not who I am."[11]

From childhood trauma to stage fright, post-traumatic stress, and continuous mounting pressures of celebrity expectations, all are relatable root causes for anxiety and panic attacks.

My first panic attack, which occurred when I was 21, was extremely traumatic to say the least. I was home from college for Thanksgiving break. It was the day after Thanksgiving, and I was hanging with friends in the city of Chicago. We had just returned to my buddy's apartment from seeing the newly released movie, *Jingle All the Way*, starring Arnold Schwarzenegger. I recall it being a strange day, though I was not exactly sure why. Perhaps it was my own subliminal conscience giving me a little heads-up warning. Whatever it was, to this day I still can't place my finger on it, but something felt off.

Once settled at the apartment, I excused myself to use the bathroom, and then suddenly without warning, my heart was

---

8 Jennifer Lopez, *True Love* (London: Celebra, 2015), 11.

9 Olivia Petter, "Emma Stone Opens Up About Anxiety and How It Gives Her High-Energy," *Independent*, August 16, 2018, https://www.independent.co.uk/life-style/emma-stone-anxiety-jennifer-lawrence-elle-interview-a8494161.html.

10 Petter, "Emma Stone."

11 Petter, "Emma Stone."

on fire and pounding out of my chest. I couldn't focus or calm myself down. I began to panic as I checked my pulse, which raced uncontrollably. The sensation kept getting worse and worse. I was sure that I was having a heart attack and was ready to call 911. All I could think about was calling my parents to say goodbye and to apologize for all my wrongdoings. I sheepishly made my way out of the bathroom and settled down in a chair. In the mix of all the commotion, I couldn't think, I couldn't breathe, and I was afraid—no, I was really scared! But, somehow over the next few minutes, the fire and pounding in my chest subsided. Everything appeared to be normal again. Or so I thought.

Over the next few weeks, I had similar episodes and several trips to the emergency room (ER). I couldn't understand what was happening to me, and I didn't feel much like myself. Each time it happened, I was sent back to my college apartment with the same diagnosis: panic attacks.

Until I received the official diagnosis, I had never heard of panic attacks. I'd heard of heart attacks of course, but that was about the extent of my medical knowledge at that time. I didn't know what to believe, but it was important to trust the doctors— after all, they were doctors, right? But was it possible for them to misdiagnose?

As it turned out, the doctors correctly diagnosed my panic attacks. What they couldn't explain were my triggering points, which led to frequent recurrences.

From the moment of my first panic attack, I became obsessed with whether a panic attack would eventually become a fatal heart attack. Any inkling of a flare-up would send me into a complete state of panic. I always followed the same order of checkpoints— placing my hand over my heart to feel my heart racing, then checking my pulse to count how many beats per minute. Next, I would wait for the heat sensation to spread quickly from my chest to the rest of my body. My breathing was the final check as I often had shortness of breath, sometimes to the point where I felt as if I was going to pass out. Then, just when I was about to call 911, suddenly my body would transition from raging panic to complete calm.

After almost every panic attack, I would have an out-of-body episode, sensing that I was on the outside looking in at myself, not knowing who I was, unable to comprehend what was happening, and in some instances, completely disoriented. It didn't make sense to me. The fact that my body would go from one extreme to the next within seconds was confusing and scary at the same time. Deep down, I knew I was physically healthy and fit, and I couldn't understand what was wrong with me.

It wasn't until I read *The Anxiety Disease* by David V. Sheehan, MD, that I was able to identify my panic attack starting points. This life-changing book helped me control my thoughts and remain calm during stressful situations. I learned how to channel my strength to overcome fears. As I dove deeper into the book, I discovered that it's the racing heart that provokes the other three sequential events: derealization, hot flashes, and fear of dying.[12] If I can regulate the racing heart, then my other panic attack symptoms remain dormant.

As I read through each chapter of *The Anxiety Disease* and did the related exercises, I learned that I had experienced panic attacks as a child. They were much smaller in magnitude back then—occurring when I was overanxious about self-confidence

---

12 David Sheehan, *The Anxiety Disease: New Hope for the Millions Who Suffer from Anxiety* (New York: Bantam Books, 1986).

and assurances from others—but it made perfect sense that they were related to my hearing impairment. By the time I finished the book, I felt I finally had a grasp on my panic attacks, and I was able to continuously apply the new techniques I'd learned. It felt good to take back control.

I'll admit, identifying the trigger points proved to be a larger challenge than I initially expected. Although I quickly pinpointed my fear of dying and the potential correlations with my hearing impairment as significant, those weren't the actual trigger points. It took some time and heavy soul-searching, but I finally identified my primary triggers, which began in childhood and continued to the present day:

1. Fear of future trauma—thinking trauma will happen again, triggering anxiety. These thoughts correlate to my fear of where and when my next panic attack will occur.

2. Post-traumatic stress—thinking about my personal traumatic events, which include flashbacks, nightmares, out-of-body experiences, and severe anxiety. These uncontrollable or subconscious thoughts correlate to my childhood, my panic attacks, the death of a loved one, and job losses.

3. Catastrophic thoughts—thinking negative thoughts about a certain situation and then expecting the worst outcome, regardless of how unlikely it is. These thoughts correlate with when I associate a particular bodily pain with thinking I will soon be diagnosed with a fatal disease; or when something goes wrong at work and I fear I might lose my job; or when I'm about to have an unpleasant confrontation and know that the other person will be upset or disappointed.

I read somewhere that the average mind thinks between 60 thousand and 80 thousand thoughts each day.[13] That's over three thousand thoughts per hour. Take a look within yourself. How many of your thoughts are negative or repetitive? There's a good chance that both you and I spend far too much mental energy dwelling on the negative and hypothetical what-if scenarios. The reality is that these negative thoughts directly contribute to panic attacks. Once you realize this, you can start noticing your negative thoughts. Then you can start shifting the way you interpret situations from a negative to a positive perspective. You can also learn to switch off your tendency to overthink things.

There isn't a cure for anxiety or panic attacks, but from my experience, the key is controlling thoughts and remaining calm during stressful, intense situations. Recognizing early symptoms and triggers are the primary steps in deterring panic attacks. Although I've learned to be prepared for panic attacks, I still experience an episode from time to time. The difference is, they are much shorter now as I quickly work to regain control.

Note: Please remember, I am not a medical professional. I am simply sharing my experiences with you with the hope that they are helpful. Always seek professional help if you are experiencing panic attacks or any related symptoms.

Your Footsteps

The National Alliance on Mental Illness offers great insights on many types of mental health conditions, each segmented into categories of overview, statistics, treatments, and support. I've read about the five predominant conditions discussed on their website:

---

13 Remez Sasson, "How Many Thoughts Does Your Mind Think in One Hour?," SuccessConsciousness, accessed April 26, 2022, https://www.successconsciousness.com/blog/inner-peace/how-many-thoughts-does-your-mind-think-in-one-hour/.

depression, anxiety, post-traumatic stress, eating disorders, and addiction.[14]

While each of these conditions is equally important, I have limited personal experience related to depression, eating disorders, or addiction; I list them here because there are those who can offer more valuable insights and shared experiences than I can. For the purposes of this particular footstep, my experiences are with anxiety and post-traumatic stress.

Anxiety is an invisible force that surrounds us every day. It can't be seen. It can't be heard. But if you've ever experienced anxiety and panic attacks, you can feel them quickly closing in. And you can't run and hide, because they follow you everywhere you go.

Life comes at you from multiple directions and at various speeds, kind of like the way a skilled boxer attacks his opponent. Overscheduled commitments, constant daily stresses at work, bills to pay, lack of sleep, and poor diet all lead to exhaustion. If you're not prepared, the unthinkable follows: anxiety. If you're fortunate, anxiety won't turn into a panic attack.

Anxiety and panic attacks can strike at any given time. Without warning, the weight of the pressure consumes your mind and body and triggers immense fear. As you continue to panic, the fear intensifies, and suddenly you lose control of everything.

Strangely enough, anxiety is often brought on by perceptions of moments that have not occurred. Throughout the day, numerous scenarios of how certain situations will play out race through your head. You stress over all sorts of potential outcomes and what will be said, how you will react, and so forth. All those potential scenarios produce stress, but what was accomplished?

---

14 "Mental Health Conditions," NAMI, accessed April 26, 2022, https://nami.org/About-Mental-Illness/Mental-Health-Conditions.

When the anticipated moment finally arrives, the outcome often contains variables you never expected, and most of the time, the result isn't nearly as bad as you initially feared it would be. Yet you placed so much focus on creating unnecessary stress and anxiety. Why is that?

The main reason we create so much internal angst is because our brains are hardwired to prepare for worst-case scenarios as a defensive mechanism for survival. This is an evolutionary process that's developed over hundreds of thousands of years. Let that sink in for a moment. Since the dawn of time, we've been stressing over things in order to survive. It's not an easy habit to shake. With practice, however, we can learn to control our mindset and change our perception of stressful situations.

Like panic attacks, anxiety can have a big impact on your daily life. The new question arises: How do you live your life free from stress? Generally, most things you worry about never happen. However, that remaining small percentage of anticipation and worry continues to weigh you down and can lead to panic attacks.

You can prepare yourself for the worst. You can anticipate and run scenarios through your mind all day long, but that's a lot of energy being consumed by stress and anxiety. Alternatively, that same energy can be directed to something you can control, like a goal or your drive to succeed and live life to the fullest.

Since 1949, the month of May has been designated as Mental Health Awareness Month. It's an opportune time to reinvest in yourself just before the meteorological change of seasons. While your New Year's resolutions might typically have addressed starting over and new beginnings, it's May when you realize those New Year's resolutions might not have come to fruition. May is the chance to hit the redo button.

I once listened to a YouTube clip that placed stressful scenarios into perspective. I can't recall the exact quote, but I'll paraphrase: Each day you encounter various stress rigors. The majority of the time you can quickly dismiss or maneuver around those rigors as you can see them coming from afar. But sometimes there are rigors missed that will quickly set you off into a tirade. But before you self-destruct, ask yourself the following question: "Do I have a five-minute problem, a five-hour problem, or a five-year problem?"

I absolutely loved that question: It makes you stop and think for a moment about which type of problem you have. Depending on the problem, you may be able to quickly bring stress down to a more manageable level. Here's my interpretation of the question to help guide you.

Five-minute problems are the most common. Examples might include getting stopped by a freight train passing through town, having someone say something you don't like, being stuck next to a crying child, or dealing with a scolding boss. Each of these examples is painful and frustrating, but if you think about it, within five minutes, the problem is over.

Five-hour problems are the next most common. Examples include enduring long flights or airport layovers, having your car break down, facing a sudden work deadline, or trying to recover a lost computer file. As with the five-minute problem, it'll soon be over.

Five-year problems are more serious and concerning but are usually rarer. Examples include chronic illness, medical troubles, financial disasters, unemployment issues, and legal matters. These long-term problems may potentially have no endpoint.

By breaking down your problem to fit one of those three time brackets, you can start to develop a sense of reality and understand the stress triggers around you. Sure, you can continue to break them down into weeks or months, but why create the added stress? Keep it simple with three time brackets and call it a day. If you follow this logic, little by little you'll see that the majority of your stress really belongs in the five-minute bracket. Let it go, and you'll be amazed how much more in control you'll feel.

Our Footsteps

If you search the internet, there are endless resources and articles available to help you self-educate on mental health conditions such as stress, anxiety, and panic attacks. However, be sure to exercise extreme caution when searching, as not all information is medically based or accurate. It's important in making decisions to consult with medical professionals who can guide you appropriately.

Prescription medications are often the first steps in treatments. However, in my opinion,* medications are short-term solutions that mask the overall mental health condition. I believe in finding the long-term solution that will enable you to successfully cope with and keep mental health issues at bay. Unless you can identify your anxiety and panic attack triggers, and work to control them—on your own—they will continue to be focal points of your life.

Note: I'm not a doctor. By no means is my opinion intended to replace that of health care professionals.

Richard Lucas, a scuba instructor who had to stop doing what he loved due to panic attacks, was quoted as saying, "I will not allow anxiety and panic to kill another day of my life. It's my life, and anxiety can't have it anymore."[15] As someone who's all too

---

15 "Anxiety, You're Not the Boss of Me," CNN, last modified February 11, 2013, https://www.cnn.com/2013/02/11/health/anxiety-first-person-irpt/index.html.

familiar with panic attacks, I really like his powerful statement about how he combats his anxiety.

When it comes to coping with anxiety and panic attacks, sometimes statements like Lucas's motivate us to do *big* things— or enough to jump-start our internal inspiration!

Below are five steps I've created over the years to help me cope when faced with stress and anxiety.

1. FOCUS ON WHAT YOU CAN CONTROL.

Don't spend your time and energy on things you can't control or on unknowns. As the saying goes, what will be will be. When you boil it down, you have some control over many anxiety-inducing factors. Here is a list of things you can control: your emotions, your actions, your diet, your exercise habits, how you treat others, how you spend money, what time you go to bed at night, who you associate with, and how you spend your free time. If you have a good grasp of these things, you'll likely experience less stress and anxiety.

2. PRACTICE MEDITATION AND REIKI.

These practices provide a successful method of release, restoring tranquility that may be blocked. Of all the different meditation alternatives available, I like Reiki best. According to Reiki.org, it's a Japanese technique for stress reduction and relaxation that also promotes healing. It is administered by "laying on hands" and is based on the idea that an unseen "life force energy" flows through us and is what causes us to be alive.[16]

3. MAKE DECISIONS BASED UPON FACTS.

Never let your emotions or opinions directly influence the outcome of a stressful situation. Gather information and make

16 "What is Reiki?," Reiki.org, accessed April 26, 2022, https://www.reiki.org/faqs/what-reiki.

your decision based on the facts at hand. This is easier said than done, but think how many times you have reacted emotionally, only to regret it once you've had some time to reflect on the overall situation.

4. ALWAYS BE TWO STEPS AHEAD—KNOW YOUR TRIGGERS.

Continually plan and reassess a situation to keep the playing field even. You can't control the weather, but you can be prepared for a sudden downpour by bringing an umbrella. When you're prepared and know your triggers, you're less likely to experience the anxiety related to having to scramble and make last-minute decisions.

5. ACCEPT THAT ANXIETY AND STRESS WILL HAPPEN.

Accept that anxiety and stress are a natural part of your life, as both occur on a daily basis. Recognize that both are critical to your body's way of protecting itself. How you initially respond to anxiety and stress will dictate their impact and how long they last.

Let's be real for a moment. Your days are filled with chaos, twists, turns, and emotions. At any given moment, it's easy to feel overwhelmed and one step away from totally losing your mind. Whether you're prone to panic attacks or not, eventually the daily chaos catches up to you. Should those inevitable trigger points start to stir, how you react will dictate whether a panic attack follows.

Here are five steps I developed to help stop panic attacks and to regain control:

1. IDENTIFY YOUR STARTING POINTS.

Distinguish whether the episode is panic attack related or something larger. Triggers include, but may not be limited to, racing heart, chest pains, difficulty breathing, tingling or numbness, and a sense of terror.

2. CLOSE YOUR EYES, SLOWLY BREATHE IN THROUGH YOUR NOSE, THEN EXHALE THROUGH YOUR MOUTH.

As you breathe in, chant "breathe," and as you exhale, "emoji." By repeating these unrelated words over and over again, your mind slowly transitions from fear to calm. Think of it as a mind redirection.

3. DRINK COLD WATER AND WASH YOUR FACE.

The coolness of the water and face washing helps restore sensation to your body. Water also alleviates dry mouth.

4. CALL A FRIEND OR LOVED ONE.

Sharing your experiences can help pinpoint triggers not yet identified during the heat of the moment. Speaking with someone who will probably reassure you that you're okay can also help calm your nerves.

5. ACCEPT THE FACT THAT YOU HAD AN EPISODE.

There is no shame in admitting that it simply happened. You had a panic attack, just like millions of other people. Anxiety and panic attacks have become more socially accepted over the years, thanks in part to increased public awareness. Understanding that you can't go backward and erase the episode, you can use it to better understand the "why" behind it. And, by accepting the fact that you just had a panic attack, you can bring closure to it, which will enable you to move forward!

Self-Reflection Footsteps

Although it may be difficult to disclose a mental health condition, celebrities who've publicly disclosed theirs serve as inspirations and help to make it socially acceptable. I have focused here on the mental health issues that I have experience with and can speak directly to, but there are many other mental health issues that need to be recognized and accepted. While "Our Footsteps" provided guidance and techniques, the following are key summary points, self-guided questions, and self-reflection exercises to help you find your own techniques to cope and live with anxiety and panic attacks.

KEY SUMMARY POINTS

1. Mental self-care plays a consequential role that involves your psychological, emotional, and social well-being as it correlates with how you think, feel, act, or respond in certain situations.

2. Anxiety and stress are a natural part of your life. Don't spend your time and energy on things you can't control.

3. Identifying trigger points can help fend off anxiety and panic attacks.

SELF-GUIDED QUESTIONS

1. How would you describe your overall mental self-care routine? What changes can you make to strengthen your routine going forward?

____

____

____

2. How much time and energy do you spend in each of the five-minute, five-hour, or five-year problem categories? What can you control? What can you let go of?

____

____

____

3. If you could release one major stress rigor, what would it be? How would you release it?

____

____

____

SELF-REFLECTION EXERCISES
1. Find your personal trigger points.

As discussed throughout the chapter, now's the moment to actually take the time to identify your trigger points. Your first instinct may be to think about what makes your blood boil or what causes your blood pressure to increase in certain situations, discussions, or anticipations.

Pivot to the invisible triggers, the ones you don't see or realize are triggering your anxiety. Examples might include having too much time to think, or letting your mind wander uncontrollably. Perhaps the media or social media play a significant role through their constant reporting of negative news, illnesses, distress, and much more. Or you may find yourself prone to hypochondria, always focusing on your health.

This exercise is not meant to create any additional anxiety, it's more of an "aha!" recognition or a starting point. If you find yourself drawing blanks or getting a bit worked up, talk with family and close friends. They may be able to provide valuable insights or observations. You might also consult with your medical provider as they may be able to pinpoint some triggers from a medical perspective. This is your opportunity for self-discovery; once you find your trigger points, write them down on a sheet of paper. This will serve as an excellent resource the next time you feel anxiety.

2.   Introduce yourself to meditation.

Whether you join a club or group or go solo, there are many health benefits in meditation. There are six popular types of practice: mindfulness meditation, spiritual meditation, focused meditation, movement meditation, mantra meditation, and transcendental meditation. Benefits include lower levels of stress; fewer asthmatic episodes; and reduced physical pain, insomnia, episodic anger, negative or irrational thinking, and anxiety.[17] In addition, meditation can help improve coping skills and focus and promote a general feeling of well-being.[18] Find a type of meditation that works best for you, one that you'll enjoy. It may be challenging at first, when you're new to the practice, but once you get the hang of it, hopefully you'll notice a sense of calmness around you!

3.   Impose a 30-, 60-, or 90-day mental health challenge.

As we discussed in chapter 1, self-imposed mental health challenges are fantastic opportunities for self-discovery and to push yourself forward. But sometimes it takes a little longer to get there. Rather than stepping into uncharted waters and feeling pressured to make immediate mental health changes, it may be better to break down your goals into 30-day periods. (There may be an episode along the way, especially when it comes to anxiety and panic attacks.) Before getting started, you'll need to track your progress. Using a whiteboard allows you to be creative, illustrating your notes as you monitor your success. This is your time to reinvest in yourself mentally and emotionally, so have fun and always remember to celebrate both small and big wins along the way!

---

17   Matthew Thorpe and Rachael Link, "12 Science-Based Benefits of Meditation," Healthline, October 27, 2020, https://www.healthline.com/nutrition/12-benefits-of-meditation.

18   Thorpe and Link, "12 Science-Based Benefits of Meditation."

Hardships, struggles, and disappointments are all part of life. The turning point is how you rebound and find opportunities to leverage your mental self-care so that you don't allow those hardships and struggles to weigh you down with fear, anxiety, and panic.

Sometimes the greatest mental battle is the one within yourself. You may not be able to control every situation, but you *can* control your mindset. The key is to avoid negative thinking or, at a bare minimum, to not let your mind wander into too many hypothetical what-if situations. While that's easier said than done, taking time to focus on your mental self-care may just be enough to keep those anxiety and panic attacks at bay and enable you to *keep those feet moving.*

CELEBRATE LIFE, NOT LOSS

There are moments in life that you will recall with exactness—remembering exactly where you were at the precise moment you first heard a piece of news. Whether the news was jubilant and gratifying or devastating and heartbreaking, they are moments you will carry for the rest of your life. Sometimes you can anticipate those moments—like when your favorite team won the championship or when you passed a difficult exam. Other times, they may be unexpected—such as a medical illness diagnosis or the passing of a loved one.

My Footsteps

The evening of March 7, 2008, was supposed to be typical. My wife, Cory, and I had been married for two and a half years, living in a suburb of Phoenix in Paradise Valley, Arizona. Our daughter, Zoey—the joy of our lives—had been born two months earlier. We were a beaming young family, proud and eager for what life had in store for us.

Cory and I were hanging individual *Z-O-E-Y* letters on the wall across from Zoey's crib in the bedroom when, suddenly, Cory became unable to communicate. Her speech slurred, and I couldn't understand what she was trying to say.

Immediately recognizing that something was wrong, I led her downstairs to the kitchen table. I asked her to write a few sentences on a piece of paper. I wanted to know if her slurred speech was a mental or physical condition, or something more. What Cory wrote down on the paper was completely unrelated to what I'd asked her. Cory's brother, who was visiting for the weekend to meet Zoey, couldn't make heads or tails of it either. Since my parents lived nearby, I called them to come over and help with Zoey while my brother-in-law and I took Cory to the hospital.

Within the hour we were sitting in a private space within the hospital's ER. Cory's speech returned to normal, and she appeared to be fine. Maybe she was dehydrated or overtired? We were first-time parents of a newborn after all. Perhaps this was normal, and I overreacted. Little did I know that our entire world was about to be turned upside down.

"The CAT scan shows a large mass," the doctor told us grimly.

Just like that, all of our lives' plans flew out the window in a single moment.

The large mass was positioned on the frontal lobe of Cory's brain, which affected her spoken language and ability to process what was being said. This explained why when we were hanging Zoey's letters on the wall, she suddenly couldn't communicate properly. It was at that precise moment that the mass pressed on the sensory areas.

Cory was formally admitted to the hospital that evening as preparations for immediate follow-up tests and surgery discussions began. She was surprisingly calm; she had been through something like this before. Two years before we began dating, Cory had been diagnosed with a lower-stage astrocytoma brain cancer, which she successfully beat.

Cory's parents were scheduled to fly down from Chicago the next day for a visit with Zoey, so as it happened, they were able to retrieve all her previous MRI scans from years earlier and bring them along.

That night at the hospital, I couldn't sleep. My mind raced. I sent Cory's brother home to get some rest, and my parents took Zoey to their house in an effort to get some sleep. Nothing seemed real. I was scared, saddened, and in a deep daze. I couldn't fully comprehend what was happening. These were surreal moments. I kept trying to wake myself up, but I was already awake. This couldn't be happening, not to us. "No way this is real," I thought. "It can't be!"

The neurosurgeon confirmed the diagnosis the next afternoon. The surgery was set for two days later. Throughout the day, there was a feeling of relief as action plans were set into motion, and everyone was optimistic. Since Cory's parents were now present, I let them take the lead as I was still in a deep daze and this was uncharted territory for me.

The night before the surgery, it was quiet, just Cory and me. We talked, we laughed, and we cried. I quickly assembled a photo album of Zoey's first two months to share—something I thought would brighten spirits. By then, it'd been 48 hours since Cory's slurring episode; she hadn't had any since. It was the last night Cory and I were together as Cory and AJ.

The anticipation of post-op news after surgery was excruciating. I'll never forget the conversation I had in the hospital hallway with Cory's neurosurgeon following her surgery. I'm still haunted by his very words: "Life expectancy, one to two years." Talk about tough news to swallow. The doctor was basically conveying that Cory had been assigned a death sentence by cancer.

Over the next 14 months, I did everything I could to save Cory. I moved us from Phoenix to Chicago so Cory could be closer to her immediate family. I lost my job twice and liquidated our savings with the hope that medical science would find a cure for Cory's cancer.

I rarely slept, spending my nights searching through medical journals and oncology reports for anything that could bring us a miracle. Each day, life as we knew it was ticktocking away. Every hour, minute, and second mattered.

Cory peacefully passed away on May 18, 2009.

We never know when our time will be up or where we'll be when it happens. We do know that when our time comes, we hope to be surrounded by those we love. Those images are the ones we keep with us forever.

When Cory passed, I was haunted by the horrors of what I'd seen and experienced. At 33 years old, what did I understand about death—about losing a spouse, becoming a widower, or being a single father? In the end, I'm able to find comfort knowing that I did everything I could for Cory. There was nothing more my strength, prayers, or adrenaline could have done to change the outcome. Cancer was bigger and more powerful. It won.

Cancer may have taken Cory's life, but I continue to stay strong for Zoey and for myself. As I write about in this book, each day that we go through in our life's journey we experience crises of various degrees. Whether it's illness, a financial setback, a relationship issue, or a problem at work—each crisis connects with one common element: If we aren't prepared, we're stopped in our tracks with no idea of where to turn next.

When I started blogging *Keep Those Feet Moving* in 2013, my goal was to help those directly or indirectly affected by cancer. However, I quickly discovered that the basic human need for inspiration and motivation goes beyond the boundaries of cancer and into all types of crises. So, if I can overcome my hearing impairment, panic attacks, and loss of a spouse, imagine what you can overcome.

Even the strong and mighty experience setbacks. It's an inescapable part of life. How we learn to knock down barriers to gain strength and to overcome the setbacks that life hands us ultimately determines the quality of our lives. Past experiences, even painful ones, can make us stronger. And if a setback knocks you down, you can build courage, strength, and determination by getting right back up again. As long as you believe that nothing can stop you, you can overcome anything.

The doctor's words about Cory's life expectancy still linger in my head all these years later—long after Cory left this world. I'll admit, I've never been the same since she passed, but instead of mourning the loss now, I choose to celebrate Cory's life every day.

THE CONSOLING POWER OF PETS

Shortly after Cory and I were married, we wanted a dog. Cory had her heart set on a small male dog. I wanted a large female Airedale because I had grown up with two of them. We settled on a female cockapoo—Myka.

Some may claim pets are just pets, but as it turned out for me, Myka was a source of strength when I needed it most. When Cory passed away, Myka would cuddle and console me in my darkest hours, often licking the tears from my face. People always asked how I coped with Cory's passing without counseling. It was Myka. And, of course, Zoey. While my tiny daughter brought laughter and joy, Myka, still acting like a puppy, brought love and companionship to both of us. She filled such a big hole in our lives that I'm not sure how I, at least, would have gotten through those first few years without her. And Myka and Zoey were inseparable—running up and down the street together, watching TV shows and romping in the living room before bedtime.

As it happened, Myka, at 15 months, was diagnosed with medical issues of her own: masticatory muscle myositis, serious stuff. Several vets suggested I put Myka down due to the medical costs and risks involved. That's when I discovered I had a lot of fight in me. I wasn't having it. I chose to fight for her, and with the right vet, Myka fought too. Aside from the myositis, through the years she endured pancreatitis, two ACL tears, a heart murmur, and kidney failure. One by one, she overcame each challenge and beat all the odds—living a good life, giving so much love, and receiving so much in return for the next 14 years. She gave us time to mourn while licking our tears. What a blessing she was.

I have no doubt that Cory blessed Myka with longevity and her fighting spirit. I hope they are romping through heaven together now.

People often wonder:

- How long is the mourning process?

- Is the feeling of losing a spouse, child, parent, or friend different from losing a beloved pet?

- At what point do you let go?

Over the past months, I've been asking myself these very same questions. Here is my take: Life is indeed a precious roller coaster ride filled with ups and downs. Remember that for every feeling of pain, agony, and defeat, there is also joy, peace, and triumph as a counterbalance. Recognizing where you are on the roller coaster will help you put life back into perspective. The truth is that where you are now is not permanent.

If you are dealing with a painful loss, hopefully you have family and friends to give you a shoulder to lean on. But as the days turn to weeks, months, and years, this external support eventually wanes. The only constant in all of this is *you*.

For years, I believed that strength comes from how you overcome challenges. But I was wrong. Strength comes from how you respond to adversity—how you rise up and stand tall and find your balance. And if you collapse under the pressure, how quickly can you rise up again? Adversity wants you to stay down and will consistently cheat to keep you grounded. Get knocked down enough times, and eventually you start to counterattack.

People—and animals too—who touch our lives provide us a great gift through joy and memories, leaving profound impressions that change our lives forever. They capture our hearts with their smiles and laughter. They become part of us as we become part of them. In the end, it's the stories we tell about them that enable them to live on.

And because their legacies carry on through time, it can feel strange when we realize they've been gone longer than the time we knew them. Detailed memories fade to become simple memories. Sounds of voices become softened. Moving images become still pictures. And when it's all said and done, you can only smile at the impact left behind.

As the days, months, and years go by, we continue to go about our lives. But there is a part of them that we will always carry with us, and no one can take that away.

Make no mistake, life is precious. How we touch the lives of others makes it that much more special. We all have a purpose. It's up to us to make the best of what we've been given. Every day is an opportunity to seize the day. To make a difference. To live life. And to celebrate life!

Your Footsteps

I've always believed that you own your life's script. During the first years of your life, you don't have much say as to how it unfolds, but as time goes on, you inherit more "script responsibilities." Sure, certain situations outside of your control may influence the direction of your next steps. But in the end, you have the ability to take control and dictate the story.

Even in adverse situations—for instance, when you receive an unexpected medical diagnosis—remember that despite what any doctor might say, you may have the capacity to write your own script. A doctor's estimation of life expectancy is only statistical. No one knows for certain when the time will come. There are too many variables that can change the matrix. Regardless of the prognosis and the unknowns ahead, there's an element not often factored into the equation: *you*!

Cancer is among the most feared medical diagnoses, ahead of Alzheimer's, heart attack or heart disease, and strokes. I've spent a lot of time researching to better understand cancer and have even formulated my own thoughts about it.

According to Dictionary.com, cancer is defined as[19]

1. "A malignant and invasive growth or tumor, especially one originating in epithelium, tending to recur after excision and to metastasize to other sites."

2. "Any disease characterized by such growths."

3. "Any evil condition or thing that spreads destructively; blight."

I prefer WebMD's definition:[20]

"Throughout our lives, healthy cells in our bodies divide and replace themselves in a controlled fashion. Cancer starts when a cell is somehow altered so that it multiplies out of control. A tumor is a mass composed of a cluster of such abnormal cells."

The key word in WebMD's definition is "altered"—meaning changed in character or composition. How and why does a cell alter and become abnormal? And why is it called "cancer"? The term was actually derived from the Greek word for "crab," perhaps due to its finger-like spreading projections—a crab has 10 legs, after all.[21] Cancer uses its crab-like legs to gravitate to an affected area and slowly circumvent the body.

However, for someone—such as myself—with unorthodox philosophical views, the word "can" in "cancer" is quite perplexing. To me, "can" conveys "enable." Personally speaking, I correlate "can" with positive action. For instance, tell me what you can do, not what you aren't able to do. I see "can" as opportunity,

---

19 Dictionary.com, s.v. "cancer (n.)," accessed April 26, 2022, https://www.dictionary.com/browse/cancer.

20 "Understanding Cancer – the Basics," WebMD, January 20, 2022, https://www.webmd.com/cancer/guide/understanding-cancer-basics.

21 Dictionary.com, s.v. "cancer (*n.*)."

growth, and achievement. If you take that mindset and tie it back to cancer, you may be able to understand why I find the entire cancer situation troubling. Each time the word is spoken, it grows because that's what the name implies. The more it's mentioned, it spreads in greater numbers. But does it truly have the power to knock you down and keep you down?

Your will power, strength, and mindset are invaluable attributes that define who you are and whether you can beat all the odds. Chances for survival are much greater for those who choose to fight their battles fiercely compared to those who give in to defeat. You are not a statistic. You are not defined by medical science, which can only take you so far. The rest is up to you and how you want to fight. Peaks and valleys will surface every day, but you've got to find the motivation to keep standing and to keep fighting.

How is my personal, indirect experience with cancer different from anyone else's? Truthfully, there's no difference. There's not a single day that goes by that I don't think about the horrors I've seen and the impact cancer has on its victims and loved ones.

However, the script I choose to write is to empower others to overcome their own setbacks to live life to its fullest potential. This is what separates my story from others. Indeed, Cory's cancer is one element of the story. I vowed not to let her cancer destroy my life or Zoey's, because we had to keep pushing on. My pledge is to help you fight your battles, so you are not alone. I will do my best to inspire, motivate, and challenge you to enable you to soar to new heights. If you can't move those mountains yourself, my goal is to help you move them. Deep down, I believe that's what Cory would have wanted.

Words can never truly describe your thoughts upon losing a loved one. Whether directly or indirectly, these losses have a profound effect on your life. While some people rise up to make a difference, others succumb to depression.

Without question, it's difficult to comprehend a loss. Whether it's a spouse, child, family member, pet, or friend, you become lost within the world. You've become so accustomed to their physical presence, and when it is no longer there, it feels weird. It's unsettling. There is a pure, awkward silence—a void, and voids can be troubling. You find yourself searching, talking out loud, staring aimlessly, trying to make sense of what's happening and how you arrived where you are, and trying to understand why you have more pain than before. Whether there are answers or not, you know you have to keep going.

The pain you feel about your loved one not coming home, not being able to talk, and not being able to be in your presence is all part of the void—disbelief or a shock that they are really gone. There is no more point of contact. There are no more opportunities. You start rethinking would've, should've, could've scenarios to justify your feelings, but in the end does that really bring comfort?

Support groups can only provide so much. They provide guidance, share words of wisdom, and serve as a physical presence. But at the end of the day, it's up to you to move things forward.

I can't take away your pain. I can't undo the past. But I can share an alternative perspective on how to cope.

Find your favorite picture of your loved one—or your pet. Stare at it affectionately. In a brief moment, you may start to crack a smile in remembrance, chuckling to yourself at a funny moment you shared. Listen closely—you can still hear their voice. Find your comfort within the loss.

Although loved ones depart from us physically, they will always be in our hearts. When you need a hug or a pick-me-up, close your eyes. Feel their arms wrapped around you. Hear their voices. And when you are ready, open your eyes. Tranquility will settle over you because you are at peace for the moment. Repeat as necessary until you find tranquility. You'll never be alone; those memories will always be with you.

I hope the readings in this book will change your perspective to help you build more confidence, to help you overcome adversity. If you're ever facing a situation where it might feel as if all hope is lost, remember that *you can*

Become so strong that no one can rise above you.

Become so tough that no one can hurt you.

Become so powerful that you become untouchable.

You have the power within you to inspire, persevere, empower, energize, achieve, and create. It all comes down to having the motivation to control your own destiny and write your life's script.

In the end, it's the stories that we tell that enable legacies to carry on. Cory left that legacy for us all.

Our Footsteps

As individuals, we each have our own personal battles. But together, we're stronger, and we now fight as one. Throughout this footstep chapter, I discussed Cory's cancer, Myka's passing, and finding strength to celebrate their lives, not to dwell on the losses. I've learned it's okay to cry. It's okay to stay in bed a little longer to collect your thoughts. But the day is upon you. Each day you awake with two choices: let the day go to waste, or take advantage of every opportunity—seize the day. Although grief and mourning are often mistakenly used interchangeably, they are different aspects of coping with loss.

Below are four steps to help cope with loss:

1. STAY IN YOUR OWN MARATHON RACE.

When it comes to coping with a loss, there really isn't a definitive time period for mourning. Some may mourn for a short period; others may turn mourning into a lifetime. Remember, it's not where you start but where you finish that matters. With that in mind, think of the mourning phase as a footrace. You've got to start at the beginning and find a way across the finish line. It doesn't matter how fast or slow you move, or what the odds are against you—what's important is that you focus your strength on getting to the finish line, which represents your loved one's life's celebration.

2. LET THE SUNSHINE COME.

Open those curtains and let the light in. Hiding in the darkness doesn't make it any easier; it's avoidance, and it only brings more pain. Hiding doesn't solve struggles, and it doesn't address grief. On the other hand, the sun's rays shining on your face feel wonderful. Think of the warmth as your loved one giving you a morning kiss.

3. TAKE MULTIPLE DOSES OF HUMOR DAILY.

The best medicine for coping with a loss is laughter. Many people struggle to have regular conversations with someone who is stricken by grief—they're at a loss for words about what to say. In reality, most people want to be inspired, motivated, and even distracted by humor and laughter.

If you find yourself stuck in grief, try to seek new adventures, share new memories, and surround yourself with funny people who make you laugh. Make a point of watching your favorite silly movies. Laughter creates happiness, which in turn helps fight grief. Imagine that the doses of laughter you're prescribing for yourself are so powerful that the feeling of grief is subdued, even if it is just for a little bit.

4. SEEK STRENGTH FROM COUNSELING, SUPPORT GROUPS, AND LOVED ONES.

You're never alone in your race. There's an entire industry dedicated to helping those directly or indirectly affected by loss. By leveraging independent counseling and support groups, you can learn valuable coping tools that give you strength to propel yourself across the finish line.

Your family and friends can be especially helpful in finding those recommended doses of humor and laughter. Identify key people whom you can trust in sharing your emotions. You'll need to lean on them from time to time.

Alternatively for some, family and friends may also add unintentional stress due to their own discomfort with a loss. This is where independent support groups and therapists enter the equation. Building a strong support network can help soften the landing as you cope.

When it comes to losing a pet, here are three steps to help ease the loss:

1. CHERISH THE MEMORY, NOT THE LOSS.

Pets bring joy and happiness. They lift moods and bring excitement and are an integral part of our lives. Therefore, grieving for a pet can be just as powerful and painful as grieving for a loved one. Without question, there is a physical void, and often we tend to focus on the void rather than the cherished memories. I've always believed it's okay to mourn for a season or two, but you can't turn a loss into a lifetime of mourning. Instead focus on those cherished memories, reminiscing about the time you spent together.

Create a pet shrine, or place your favorite photo on display. Although the pet may no longer be there physically, its presence can still be felt spiritually. Love is an emotional, powerful feeling. It'll always be there if you embrace it and let it in. Those memories will follow you wherever you go. As I've done with Myka, designate a favorite spot or something pictorial, like a rainbow, to honor your beloved pet. When you see it, a natural smile will form as you are merely saying hello.

2. SEEK SUPPORT THROUGH FAMILY, FRIENDS, OR PROFESSIONALS.

Asking for support is a sign of strength. It shows a sense of commitment to your overall well-being. Grief is not easy, as there is sadness, anger, and a sense of emptiness inside. There aren't many who can shrug it off and carry on with a business-as-usual mentality. It's perfectly acceptable to seek guidance, to talk through your feelings, to learn coping strategies, and to be surrounded by those who understand the loss. While family and friends may be great at helping you cope, trained professionals can offer coping strategies that often resonate. They offer a subtle alternative and can help guide you through the grieving process. Your mourning doesn't weaken the need for guided support. Life has so much to offer, and with a little help, together you can continue to cherish those moments with your pet.

3. DON'T POUR SALT ON AN OPEN WOUND.

Obviously, that's a figure of speech, but the context is relatable in how grief settles in. There's an open wound, which takes time to heal. Anything poured on the wound will sting and bring discomfort. Depending on your personality, you may quickly replace a beloved pet with another. Sometimes during grief, you make decisions based on impulse and emotion because the pain is too great. In some instances, a replacement pet can soften the landing. Or you may wait for a season or two, then decide. There's no right answer to how long to wait; however, over the years, I've learned not to make decisions during the mourning phase as you may not be in the right mental state or frame of mind to do so. In the end, you don't want to settle on something you weren't truly prepared for or didn't want initially.

Self-Reflection Footsteps

Anytime there's a loss, the physical void is the most difficult part to comprehend. The loss of touch, voice, and the ability to create new experiences together is unsettling and deeply emotional. The good news is that despite how you are feeling, you can actually do something special to preserve your loved one's legacy. Although it may involve creativity with various degrees of difficulty at first, trust me, you won't regret it. The following are some key summary points, self-guided questions, and self-reflection exercises to help you celebrate the life of loved ones.

KEY SUMMARY POINTS

1. While loved ones, including beloved pets, depart from you physically, they will always be with you in your heart.

2. When it comes to mourning, stay in your own marathon race, as it's not where you start or how fast you go that matters; it's where you finish that is most important.

3. Mourning focuses on the *why* aspect. Celebrating the life focuses on the *where* aspect.

SELF-GUIDED QUESTIONS

1. Where can you draw strength from during challenging moments? How can you use it to take steps forward?

____

____

____

2. If a loved one were to write a story or describe your legacy, what would you want them to write or say?

____

____

____

3. How can you celebrate the life of a loved one? What can you do to capture those fond memories?

____

____

____

SELF-REFLECTION EXERCISES

1. Write children's books.

When I speak about hospice care, I always recommend embracing the moments you have together with your loved one. Instead of sitting in awkward silence or misery, you can create fun activities. For example, reading children's books together (such as *The Cat in the Hat*) can bring back cherished memories and help to create lasting ones. You enjoyed these books as a child and can still enjoy them. That's a beautiful memory to share together again. You can even frame the book with a photo or a note, capturing your time together.

The same concept can be applied in helping you celebrate the life of a loved one. Write a children's book starring your loved one as the main character. It can be a story of your lives together, or a fairy tale. Be creative. Take your readers through the story. This is a great way to keep your loved one's legacy alive!

2. Create and fulfill a bucket list.

Bucket lists are designed to help us stimulate and enjoy life, creating an opportunity to fulfill desires, passions, and curiosities. Unfortunately, the items on bucket lists often never get checked off because the list is considered more of a mere wish list than one to actually be fulfilled. Remember all those ideas, fantasies, and places you and your loved one spoke about in the past but just never got around to fulfilling? This is your chance to create an actual bucket list, then slowly cross off each item upon fulfillment. The bucket list serves a dual purpose, one for you and one for your loved one. What was once a dream can be a reality, something I bet you never thought was possible.

In the end, you can mourn the loss or continue to celebrate the life. I have found that those who mourn focus their energy on the *why* aspect—questions without answers—which prevents closure. Those who continue to celebrate the life focus on the *where* aspect. Where do I go from here? Where does my next journey take me? Life is fragile and can be taken at any time. As you celebrate life each day, the days will be longer and filled with more wonderful memories. That's how you *keep those feet moving.*

5

ENGAGE AND SPEND QUALITY TIME WITH YOUNG MINDS

Children have vivid dreams of greatness: dreams to become superstars or popstars, travel the world, or perform before thousands of screaming fans. Dreams to be like their parents who are significant role models. Dreams to become immortal, iconic figures who accomplish things never seen before.

As we age, sometimes we pass the idea of living our childhood dreams onto our own children with the same passion, enthusiasm, and hope that one day they will follow in our footsteps. If we are not careful, we may find we've pushed our children too much to live *our* dreams. When this happens, those dreams quickly diminish. As hard as it is, it's important to remind ourselves daily to enjoy our precious moments with our children and to not get caught up with living our former dreams. Instead, close your eyes for a moment to take it all in. Let children be children. Go ahead; have fun—smile, laugh, and be silly. We can engage in their excitement and hope, but remember—children are children only once. They have their *own* dreams.

My Footsteps

As a child, I had dreams of becoming a professional soccer player. I also wanted to become an accountant just like my father. And I wanted to get married and have children. Of course, I would have to date first. In any case, long before I chose to attend college at the University of Florida, I had my sights set on the University of Southern California. But somewhere along the way, those dreams changed and faded into oblivion.

As part of the senior year tradition, as a blurb for the high school yearbook, you're often asked to speculate where you'll be in 10 years. Years later, you read what you and other classmates wrote and laugh because the majority of the predictions weren't even close. My prediction—to own a professional sports team at the age of 28. Yep, not even remotely close! I'm not really sure what I was thinking when I wrote that blurb.

If, back then, someone was to have predicted that 15 years later, I'd be a widower and single father, it would have been unthinkable. I mean, what kind of prediction is that? But the truth is, the unthinkable became my reality.

I rarely spoke about being a widower because I preferred to lead a private life. I didn't want people to treat me differently because I lost a spouse or was raising my daughter on my own. It simply wasn't in my nature to complain about my situation or disclose personal aspects about my life. No surprise there, as I never spoke about my hearing impairment either.

But over the years, people asked me what it's like being a widower and raising a daughter on my own. There are many perceptions about what life's like after the loss of your spouse, but here's my take:

1. WE ARE NEVER TRULY ALONE.

Our spouses may have physically left us, but they are angels who are still among us. You may not see them, but you can feel them. They guide us through, allow us to gain strength, and watch over us. Throughout our dreams each night, these angels send little messages to decipher. Sometimes the message may not be clear, or perhaps it seems meaningless, but there is communication with the other side.

2. WE DON'T PRETEND TO HAVE ALL THE ANSWERS.

It's not easy to explain the sequence of events that led to the tragedy, nor do we understand why it had to happen. Sometimes not knowing answers brings comfort as some things are better left unknown or without explanation. In retrospect, the pain may be too great to share or completely blocked out as part of the coping process.

3. DEPRESSION CAN BE REAL AND SERIOUS.

There's a physical void in our lives. Whether we spent years caring for a sick spouse or whether it was sudden, the initial shock of the physical void can easily spiral into a depressive state. Let us cry and let us mourn. We will be okay. Sometimes we just need a good cry and some time alone.

4. WE ARE SMARTER AND STRONGER THAN WE LOOK.

Just because we may dress down or might be disheveled, it doesn't mean we're falling apart. It's our way of finding comfort within ourselves; for the time being, looks are not important.

5. WHILE WE APPRECIATE SUPPORT WHEN FRIENDS CHECK IN, PLEASE DON'T START OFF BY ASKING IF WE'RE OKAY.

No, we are not. But it doesn't mean we have to talk about it all the time. Instead let's do something fun, get out of the house, or get some fresh air. Talking about it brings back memories. Although the memories are special, right now we need activities that keep our heads clear.

6. WE DIDN'T JUST BECOME RICH.

If we're lucky, financial planning may help us offset expenses associated with medical bills and funeral costs. Anything left over may go toward other expenses to make up for the loss of income. The idea of suddenly inheriting a windfall generally applies to the movies. It's not reality. If anything, we incur more expenses after all is said and done.

7. WE NEVER STOP LOVING OUR SPOUSE.

Some widow/ers quickly find new relationships, while others may struggle. We all have our own way of mourning and moving on. Please don't judge anyone on the timing of their dating. When the moment is right, we will take a step forward. In some instances, we may prefer to be alone, and that is okay too.

8. WE LIVE THROUGH OUR CHILDREN.

The children are our legacies. As we continue to age, the stories shared and passed down are for the children and perhaps grandchildren to remember us by. Children bring enjoyment, excitement, and a little chaos too. These moments keep us alive and laughing.

9. MEMORIES DO FADE OVER TIME.

Many memories are associated with a person's physical presence. After they are gone, little by little, specific details fade until eventually we are left with only still images.

10. LIFE DOES GO ON, AND SO DO WE.
Over time, we learn to cope, stretch our wings, and fly again. And when we look back, we smile at how far we've come. No one said it would be easy. There are challenging days and good days. What's most important is how we've grown from the experiences.

Life as a single father certainly has its highs and lows. Almost always, the reactions I received from others about how I was doing as a father were heartfelt and genuine, but humility tells me I just did the best I could under the circumstances. I wish I could have done more for Zoey, who lost so much. Because of that, I have a tendency to overcompensate and go above and beyond what is usually expected. I cherish the special bond that exists between us. I can only hope others enjoy the same passion and joy with their children as I do with my daughter.

However, there are moments when children ask tough questions. Often, at that moment, we find ourselves in a quandary, deciding whether to give a truthful, straightforward answer or to sugarcoat in the interest of protecting them.

When Zoey was younger, she asked recurring, tough questions about how her mother died. Questions of how and why she got cancer, why medicine couldn't save her, and specific details of how she died. With each answer, I could see that she pondered further, trying to make sense of it all. It was natural; she was at the inquisitive age. She'd come to learn that her home life was not the same as that of her peers at school. She now realizes that girls in her situation—who grow up with only a father—develop a unique perspective on life.

I've been open with Zoey about her mother's illness and passing, especially during the month of May when we mark Cory's anniversary date. Often, the dialogue centers on hypothetical what-ifs or just shared feelings of sadness. Sometimes the truth hurts, but knowing how to tell the story can often soften the landing.

For instance, anytime I described cancer, I used the term "illness" rather than "sickness." For a child, there needs to be a distinction between the two. I didn't want Zoey to worry every time she got sick or heard the word "sick" and correlate it with her mother. Better word choices enabled me to fully describe the illness and sequence of events that followed. They also helped me maintain my emotional composure as I spoke.

Sometimes when I put Zoey to bed, there was an eerie silence surrounding us. As I watched her fall asleep, tears welled in my eyes as I thought about the fact that she never really knew her mother. Other than through stories and pictures, she has no real recollections, no memories of her own. Instead, she relies on others to keep her mother's legacy alive. She's a strong little girl, but I cannot imagine what she goes through each day with the loss. Perhaps that is why I choose to have an open relationship with her—talking about everything—even if that means answering the tough questions.

Some professionals and readers may disagree with my rationale of full disclosure, but that's okay. I respect that. It's not about right and wrong. We all have our own values and our own ways of coping. Whatever brings comfort I believe should be deemed acceptable.

Another thing that happens when you're a single father raising a daughter is that you often get caught in tight spots, such as entering a men's room with no changing tables. Or when shopping for clothes, you get stuck trying to match the proper tops with bottoms. Or you're the only father attending kids' birthday parties. Let me tell you, at those parties there's way too much gossip—not the best place for a dad!

Over the years I've learned to appreciate both maternal and paternal roles. Obviously, I can never replicate the true maternal role, but I do make an honest attempt. However, there are moments when Zoey asks mom-related questions that I struggle to answer:

Zoey: "Daddy, can you French braid my hair this morning for school?"

Me: "Sure … what's a French braid?"

Zoey: "Daddy, what's a tampon?"

Me: "Uh, we'll discuss that another time."

Zoey: "Where does it go?"

Me: "Uh, um … we'll discuss that another time too."

Zoey: "Why do girls wear makeup?"

Me: "To look beautiful."

Zoey: "When can I wear it?"

Me: "When you are older."

Zoey: "So I have to wait until I am older to be beautiful?"

Me: "Uh, I don't have an answer for this one."

Looking back, probably the correct response would have been, "You are beautiful now; there's no need to wear makeup!"

As a parent, moments like these are truly precious, especially when children catch us off guard with humorous questions or statements. Of course, I'm sure I used my fair share of dad jokes along the way. I look forward to laughing about them together with

Zoey one day when she's old enough (which is scarily approaching faster than I could have imagined).

Despite the heartaches and pains that come with coping as a widower, I embraced the role of being a single father. Zoey and I have shared many joyous and memorable occasions together, just the two of us. Outside of our house, I'm often more reserved and serious natured. At home, I'm silly and loose. Why? Because I love my daughter more than anything, and I will do anything to see her smile and hear her laughter. It's these genuine, heartfelt moments that I wouldn't trade for anything.

I deeply appreciate that Zoey will be a child only once and that she needs me as much as I need her. There will be a time in a few years when she'll be off to college, and she'll make her own choices in life afterward. Until then, I will take advantage of every opportunity to play, hang, cuddle, go places, and be together. Her smile and laugh are infectious and always brighten my day!

If I have one regret, it's that I wish I had consistently taken more photos and videos of Zoey and me together from the time she was a baby up to her teens. Sometimes I'd be so caught up playing, chasing her around the playground, or just hanging out that I would forget to capture those moments. Although I can't turn back time, I can make a conscious effort to take those selfies going forward.

Children are not perfect, and neither are we as parents. For those moments when I feel run down, frustrated with never-ending bedtime routines, and unhappy about an occasional attitude problem, I remind myself daily how fortunate I am; I know there are many parents who would love to have the same opportunity I do.

When our loved ones leave us, memories and stories are often all we have left. This is why I make sure Zoey knows that her mother loves her very much and watches from the heavens above. There are photos of Cory in Zoey's room to remind her that her mother is close by and in our hearts. I've often told Zoey, "If you want to talk to Mommy, she will listen. If you want Mommy to be with you, ask her to join you." And I admit, on more than one occasion I've had to use the "Mommy would agree with Daddy that it's time for bed" card!

I believe it's important to keep Cory's memory alive and to celebrate her life. I tell Zoey she has the best of both worlds: Daddy protects her here on Earth, and Mommy protects her from above. Mommy is our angel. We miss her every day. I don't know if I will ever fully recover from the loss, but I do know that Cory watches over us and protects us from harm. I think the simple fact that Zoey knows this helps her make sense of the situation. And it helps keep Cory's memory alive each day as we continue to celebrate her life.

Over time, I've learned that life as a single father is rewarding and that there's never a dull moment. But if you tweak your game just enough, you may get some quick wins to offset any challenges that come along with it. I'll admit, I've caught some lucky breaks. And for that, I am very grateful!

If you go back to the beginning of this footstep chapter, when I mentioned how we sometimes live our childhood dreams through our children, this may be considered a prime example. When Zoey was seven years old, she wanted to play soccer. As a former player myself, I was ecstatic. I could hardly contain myself. I immediately purchased her first cleats, shin guards, soccer ball, and bag. Next, she chose her uniform number. I couldn't wait for her to play.

Naturally, I dreamed of coaching her and teaching her all aspects of the game, transforming her into a star. But respecting my parenting boundaries, I decided it would be best to let her simply play the game, not to coach.

I loved watching Zoey play, but I'll admit I had to bite my lip and refrain from being a sideline father. During the game, she seemed more interested in rhythmic dancing and perfecting certain dance routines than chasing the soccer ball. After all, she was seven years old, and that's what girls do, right? Occasionally she did get a foot on the ball, but she was more excited when she danced around in her position afterward as an act of celebration for touching the ball. By the time the games ended, I'd bloodied my lip from biting it so hard.

As the soccer season waned and the final game was in its closing minutes, it was like watching the end of an era. Zoey may never play soccer again, but who knows? Maybe she will get the itch later in life. I learned that certain dreams are not for everyone. Instead, it's the enjoyment Zoey and I shared during the season that mattered most. Years later, I still get a kick out of it and smile because she played.

Your Footsteps

Life continues to come at you hard. For every achievement, triumph, and fortunate break, there are disappointments and setbacks—not to mention missed opportunities. Although these inconsistencies can be discouraging, they are part of life. The difference is how you rise up.

There is a fight in all of us. No matter how many times you get knocked down, you rise back up. The daily grind pushes you to your limits. The question is whether you can truly withstand the punches.

There is inspiration everywhere you go. There is empowerment in every step you take. There is motivation to accomplish what you can.

For every obstacle, the course is one giant maze with many alternatives. For every barrier, there is an opportunity to knock it down. Your strength lies deep within you.

You can succeed in getting what you want. You can succeed in anything you do because, even when you fail, you at least made some progress and learned something new along the way. You will prevail. How? Just believe in yourself. If you believe you have the strength to move mountains and soar to new horizons, then limits can't define you. You define those limits. Perception is everything.

There is a difference between your perception and how others perceive you. This helps to explain how one person uses a devastating tragedy to make a difference, while another person may fall apart into a depressive state. There truly aren't right or wrong approaches; it's just how one responds to adversity.

When Cory passed away, family members and friends assumed I would fall apart emotionally and not be able to handle the responsibilities of being a single father. That's what the overall perception was of grief, and I was considered a young widower at the age of 33. But in reality, it was the opposite.

At Cory's funeral, I stood tall, poised. I refused to cry or display emotion, as I needed to remain strong for Zoey and myself and everyone who attended. There was a sense of calm that stood with me, protecting me. I could sense it; I knew exactly what I needed to do. I felt Cory's presence next to me.

When you lose a loved one, whether it's a spouse, a child, a parent, a family member, or even a friend, it takes an emotional, mental, and physical toll on you. People are quick to judge and place labels on you whether as a way of mourning the loss or just merely spreading gossip. In my case, I was labeled as a widower raising a little girl by those who knew my story. At the time, I was faced with a very difficult challenge, one that I was determined to battle through.

That was me. It's different for everyone, but here's what I can offer you from my experience: Never back down from a challenge, no matter how difficult it is and no matter the odds or the pain. Close your eyes. Feel the rush of adrenaline in reaching new heights. Focus on your thoughts. Stay determined. Strive to push yourself even further and test unlimited boundaries. There is no failure, only achievement and success.

Don't ever let anyone tell you that you are not good enough, that you can't do it, that it's impossible, that you don't have the strength or skills, or worse, that there is nothing more that can be done. Although those words do get spoken, in the end, it's not for anyone else to decide, dictate, or determine your path.

There will be critics. There will be unfavorable outcomes. They are part of life. How you respond makes all the difference. It begins with perception and the ability to move forward. Once you are able to separate the emotional aspects from the challenge presented, you can begin to see open pathways ahead. It may not be easy, and you may have stumbling blocks along the journey, but the reward at the end is far greater than imagined.

Never be afraid to achieve success in life. Only you can make greatness happen. Only you can create those miracles you dream of. The greater the challenge, the harder you'll have to work. If something isn't working correctly, change it. Keep changing the formula until you get it right. Never stop to rest. One day you'll look back and be proud of your accomplishments. You'll see how far you've come. But don't look backward too long—you still have more personal greatness to achieve ahead.

The same goes for children. As a parent, you do your best for your children. You address meltdowns, and you comfort fears. You protect your children from harm. You laugh. You cry. You act silly. You get upset. You scratch your head. You give them everything, because they are the light of your life.

The day Zoey was born, everything I thought I knew about raising a child went out the window. Suddenly I was looking for a manual from the hospital providing guidelines and suggestions for every type of scenario that potentially could arise. Imagine my bewilderment in discovering that no such manual exists. Although you read all the literature and believe you are fully prepared, nothing can truly prepare you for the moments after a child is born.

As children grow, you begin to teach them family and life values—values you hope they will incorporate into their life later on—or at least attempt to! Of the many values I taught Zoey, generosity was one of my favorites. The impact that generosity leaves behind is as self-rewarding as it is appreciated. It doesn't have to be about money; volunteering time also serves a divine purpose. Too often in life you look for a rate of return in things—like recognition or prestige—but in doing so, ask yourself, "Where's the self-reward?" Generosity comes in a myriad of variations. Each day is an opportunity to teach values, and teaching your children is that much more special.

Be mindful, because sometimes values can be taken to the extreme. In 2013, Zoey was in kindergarten, and I couldn't figure out why her lunch account was autocharging every two days. I looked at her purchases online and was astonished to see multiple lunches purchased, sometimes additional side items too. I contacted the school to inquire and was informed that Zoey was buying lunches for all her new school friends. Later that evening, I sat her down and asked why she was buying lunches for her friends. She responded that I always buy meals for my friends and that she wanted to do the same. I spent the remainder of the night explaining the true art of generosity and how to apply it conventionally. (It was either that or I would have provided lunch for the entire school indefinitely!)

As a parent, you are a role model for your children. Despite their infatuation with celebrities and athletes, you are still their most influential individual. There will be ups and downs, twists and turns, just like a roller coaster. Shrug it off. Choose your battles. Not everything has to be a crisis. Love your children unconditionally and embrace them every moment you can. And yes, even when the next meltdown occurs, it's okay. It'll eventually subside. Either that or you'll join them in the meltdown.

Values will come and go throughout life. And as we age, our children remind us of those values we once taught. In the end, all you can do is smile.

Life as a parent is exciting, rewarding, chaotic, and head scratching. Any free time you thought you might have is quickly consumed by children's activities. Then there's the constant worrying about whether our children are safe, if they're eating properly, if they are happy, or when the next meltdown might occur. And despite all of these stresses and concerns, you wouldn't trade being a parent for the world.

Some people claim that there aren't any secrets to being a parent. You can spend countless hours reading books and engaging in discussions about childhood behavior and psychology—and these experiences may provide helpful insights. But I have found that in the end—as with most things—logic, reasoning, and intuition usually prevail. And there is actually a secret to successful parenting—it's called *spending quality time and having fun with your children.* Laugher, smiles, silliness, all the fun times.

At the end of the day, recount the wonderful memories you've shared together. If you're lucky, you may have captured a few in photos or videos. Enjoy the experience now, because children grow up quickly. Before you know it, they are grown, and you are reminiscing, wishing they were young again, holding onto their beloved little treasures—security blankets, stuffed animals, pajamas—the little treasures children value most in this world. They feel immune while their treasure is in their possession. As children grow older, naturally they progressively let go of those things, but they will always feel something special about those little treasures, even years later into adulthood.

Take a moment to think back to your most prized treasure growing up. Remember how it protected you from harm—all your scary thoughts and fears suddenly vanished when you held it. For a brief moment, you were untouchable, free from stress, free from pain. Sometimes the warmth and comfort of your little treasure was all you needed to feel happy and loved. Admit it, you can't help but smile when thinking about it again.

When Zoey was younger, she loved her stuffed animal Puppy. Wherever she went in the house, Puppy was not too far behind. In car rides, Puppy sometimes rode along. Through sleepiness, anxiety, and sadness, Puppy was always there to comfort. Even when Zoey wanted to talk about Cory, Puppy was clenched against her chest. I can't tell you how many times Puppy has gone through the washer and dryer. Little by little, Puppy lost her fur. I used to think it was not because of all the washings, but because Zoey held onto Puppy so tightly. It was her comfort zone.

Growing up, I had a small stuffed animal, Baby Bear, that I cherished. I also had a baby blanket that my mother made. I've long since given both to Zoey as a tangible part of my childhood that she'll pass along to the next generation if she wants to. Baby Bear sits on Zoey's bed, and every time I look at it, I have fond memories of my past. I hope one day when Zoey grows up, she can look at Puppy and think about how much she loved her stuffed animal and how it became a part of her. Through thick and thin, Puppy was always there for her, protecting her. And whenever she may be sad or lonely in the future, you can be sure that Puppy will be right by her side.

Though insignificant to others, the little treasures we value have no substitutes. They will always be a part of our lives and serve us well. Other moments that are forever cherished and remembered as if they happened yesterday may involve certain events that truly touched our hearts. A favorite of mine was when Cory called me at work excitedly.

"The kid is walking!" she exclaimed.

Due to Cory's deteriorating condition, she had started calling Zoey "kid." I don't know if it was because her memory was fading to the point that she couldn't remember our daughter's name, or perhaps it was just easier to say. Either way, Cory was there to see Zoey taking her first steps at 16 months. Cory was so excited and proud that day. She couldn't wait to call me right away.

Two weeks later, Cory passed away. I find comfort knowing she lived long enough to see Zoey walk. I think I may have a video of it somewhere.

Our Footsteps

I've continually believed that life is what you make of it. Nothing goes as planned, and there will always be unforeseen challenges and setbacks. While my story is shared by others who faced similar tragic losses, it still feels unreal that the unthinkable became a reality.

Earlier in the chapter, I discussed my take on what it is like being a widower and raising a child as a single parent. I know I don't have all the answers on raising Zoey, but that's okay—it's a lifelong process, and I'm still learning. That said, here are my top five steps for succeeding as a single parent. I would like to think that they apply to dual-parent households as well.

1. KEEP TO A SCHEDULE FOR NAPS AND BEDTIME.

With everything else, just go with the flow, but by sticking to a consistent nap and bedtime routine, you can easily accomplish your tasks and plan for fun activities without overscheduling. Plus, this schedule minimizes the risk of meltdowns. With a little luck, you may even find some personal downtime to recharge.

2. ALWAYS SCHEDULE QUALITY PLAYTIME.

I truly believe that there is nothing more important than spending uninterrupted, quality playtime together. The bonds you'll create with your children will last a lifetime. When you're fortunate enough to have these times, cherish them. This your opportunity to laugh, be silly, and go on adventures—even if it's just going to the park, you can explore uncharted fantasies. The more playtime you have together, the more memories and photo opportunities you'll create.

3. MAKE YOUR CHILDREN YOUR FIRST PRIORITY—NO EXCEPTIONS.

While work and personal obligations may take temporary precedence, let your children know that they are your first priority and reinforce it. Children who grow up in a single-parent household can find it tough, because they will often compare their situation with that of their friends. But when your children know they are the *most* important thing in *your* life, they'll feel a sense of security, comfort, and plenty of love.

4. BE PREPARED FOR AWKWARD QUESTIONS.

Everyone wants to know how you became a single parent, so be prepared to talk about it. Depending on the situation and your personality, you may decide to respond minimally or go into full detail. Remember that people ask questions because it's basic human nature for them to be curious—they aren't trying to be condescending. Knowing that will make it a lot easier for you to respond.

5. THERE'S NO BLUEPRINT FOR PARENTING.

Families, friends, coworkers, and even strangers will tell you what you are doing wrong or what you should be doing. That's okay. You don't have to listen to them. In the end, just go with the flow, live and learn. Blueprints are great for architecture, not parenting!

Self-Reflection Footsteps

One of my favorite movies growing up was *Ferris Bueller's Day Off* starring Matthew Broderick. There is an iconic scene where the main character declares, "Life moves pretty fast. If you don't stop and look around once in a while, you could miss it."[22] Not only is the quote relatable to most anything you do, but it's also perfect when it comes to children.

Below are key summary points, self-guided questions, and self-reflection exercises to help you build many wonderful memories with your children.

---

22 *Ferris Bueller's Day Off*, directed by John Hughes (1986; U.S.; Paramount Pictures, 1999), film.

KEY SUMMARY POINTS

1. There aren't any secrets to parenting, but logic, reasoning, and intuition usually prevail.

2. Make your children a top priority: schedule time to play, hang, cuddle, go places, and be together every day.

3. Go ahead, have fun—smile, laugh, and be silly. A child's smile and laugher will always brighten your day.

SELF-GUIDED QUESTIONS

1. How have personal challenges and setbacks changed your life? How have you learned and grown?

____

____

____

2. What's your greatest challenge as a parent? How can you turn the challenge into an opportunity?

____

____

____

3. What positive changes can you make to engage more with your children? How can you spend more time together?

____

____

____

____

Self-Reflection Exercises

1. Disconnect from all technology.

Who or what gets your best energy? Where is most of your energy spent? Work? Family? Friends? Children? How about technology? Think of the amount of time that you spend daily on your phone, tablet, or computer. Are you constantly checking Facebook and Instagram in anticipation that you may have missed a post or to see who liked your recent post? Is this the best way to spend your energy?

As we navigate this technological world, it's no surprise that devices sometimes consume our best energy and children become secondary. We need to switch that—flip-flop your best energy from devices to your children. Actually schedule time in your busy day to fully engage with them. Turn off all your devices, and put them away. No more work emails. No more personal emails, texts, or calls. Let your children know that they are most important and that there is nothing greater than your time spent together. And you know what? I think they'll enjoy your uninterrupted time together too.

2. Create a family heirloom.

When you first think of family heirlooms, your thoughts might immediately gravitate to fine jewelry, timepieces, or furniture passed down from generation to generation. Why not create your own family heirloom with your children that you can pass down as a new tradition? And if you already have existing heirlooms, why not have multiples?

Creating scrapbooks and photo albums are nice traditions and beloved, but let's go deeper! Perhaps you can share your most prized treasure from when you were growing up— children might like the idea of joining treasures together. Create a new recipe and handwrite it together—it will not only be sentimental for you and your children in years to come but for future generations too. Or you might create an art masterpiece together and sign it when it's completed—or perhaps a series of masterpieces to form a collection. The beauty of art is that it can be anything the children imagine. Regardless of the heirloom selected, this is a beautiful activity to engage in with your children.

3. Slow down to embrace time together.

You speed through life going from place to place. One moment here, the next there. You continually look ahead to the next stop on the list. From family obligations to work to your children's doctor appointments—it's nonstop. No wonder you may feel stressed and run down all the time. You are trying to maintain control and continually juggle every commitment and distraction around you. The slightest disruption can send you into a downward spiral, which in turn often gets taken out on children. It's not personal, it's not intentional, but it happens because, by the end of the day, you are simply worn out.

Each day is a gift—embrace it. Feel blessed for what you have. It's okay to slow down once in a while and enjoy a little "me time." But if that me time becomes a constant fixture instead of time with your children, you may want to rethink your priorities. Every time you tell your children you're too tired or just not in the mood, it hurts their feelings as they desperately want to engage with you. Instead, push yourself to take the extra moments to engage, to spend time together, or to talk about fantasies. Remind yourself throughout the day that you are very fortunate for the time you have with your children, and there are many other parents who would love to have the same opportunity that you do. The more you practice that notion, the more you will be pleasantly surprised how the sweet sounds of laughter will soothe your long, tiring day!

I understand that not all family dynamics and situations are similar. And families faced with personal challenges certainly do not have it easy; after all, mourning the loss of a loved one and raising children are huge challenges. But one way I look at it is that families that endure personal challenges together can develop a special bond. In the end, it's what you make of it and how you respond to adversity. Some rise and flourish. Others succumb to defeat. Of the many stories out there, mine's no different other than the fact that I chose to *keep those feet moving*.

NAVIGATE THE DATING PUZZLE

If you've gone on a date lately, you probably know how much the dating process has evolved over the years. If you haven't, that's okay too—you're quite lucky! Today, traditional dating is considered obsolete because asking someone out on a date has become informal, replaced by "hanging out." Couples are more open about their dating desires, sometimes dating multiple people at once. People are willing to go Dutch and split the costs. Technology has played a significant part in that because it's easier to connect through emails, text messaging, and dating apps.

Despite the modern changes, dating still isn't easy. I think of it like putting together a jigsaw puzzle. In order to assemble the puzzle successfully, you have to work diligently to make all the pieces (especially the more challenging ones) fit perfectly. It may take some compromise on your part, or perhaps you might need to change your expectations to help make those pieces align better.

However you do it, dating is not easy to navigate.

My Footsteps

"I will never date again, nor will I ever remarry!"

I spoke these very words not long after Cory passed. I just couldn't see myself with anyone else, nor did I want to go through the "dating interview" process all over again. I also couldn't comprehend going through the pain of losing someone I love for a second time.

It is often said that time heals wounds, and sure enough, over time those defiant words of mine softened, and the concept of dating again became more feasible. Only this time, dating as a widower and single father was much different from dating as a young bachelor. Generally speaking, you learn to crawl before you can walk, and dating is exactly the same concept.

In high school, I wasn't popular or part of the "cool" crowd, but I had a small group of friends. I struggled to attract girls because I was known for my hearing impairment, and girls just weren't interested in dating me. I may have set a record for the most prom rejections at one school—which was eight by the way—but I did go to prom with a friend of mine who attended another school. Throughout my high school years, I worked hard to fit in, determined to change the perceptions of my peers. I guess you could say I just wanted to be well liked and accepted without being labeled. I was troubled by peer-perception barriers and social obstacles, which constantly tested my dating stamina. Upon graduation, I elected to suppress my high school memories and simply move on.

College opened my eyes to new aspects of dating, and that carried over into my young bachelor days. I reinvented myself, finding a new sense of confidence and popularity. Although no one actually said as much to me, I'm sure some people suspected something was a bit off with my hearing as I may not have answered a question here or there correctly, or I may not have heard people calling my name. In my mind, since I never publicly disclosed my hearing impairment, no one knew anything about my past. Looking back, I was only fooling myself.

When I met Cory on October 30, 2002, I knew instantly that I would marry her. A spark ignited inside of me as we had the perfect dinner date. I don't like the taste of fish, but when Cory offered me a bite of her salmon, I readily accepted. The fact that she got me to eat a tiny piece of fish on our first date left a long-lasting impression—which only confirmed that she was the one.

Cory not only touched my life, but she also touched the lives of everyone who knew her. She brought joy and laughter. She was witty and had the kindest soul. From the moment we met until the moment she closed her eyes one final time, we were inseparable. When I finally disclosed my hearing impairment to her, she brushed it off as if it was no big deal. It didn't matter to her; she loved me for *who* I was, not *what* I was.

We were married on July 10, 2005, in a beautiful wedding. As we danced the night away, surrounded by family and friends, I finally achieved my lifelong dream—married! After all those rejections, another chapter was finally closed. I was a proud, married man with the love of my life. Life couldn't be any better.

Within a year after we were married, I made a difficult decision to leave a prestigious anti-money-laundering job in Chicago and relocate to Phoenix. I loved my job and the entitlement that came with it, but my position had peaked, the bank was on the verge of being sold, and the prospects of starting a family became real.

Phoenix afforded me the opportunity to work with my father and learn a new trade. Remember, when I was younger, I wanted to be an accountant just like my father. I checked the box of another lifelong goal as I believed this relocation provided the right opportunity for us. Although Cory wasn't 100% on board, she supported me and the decision. Still, there was one overlooked element—an element that I never even considered. The facts were there; I just flat out missed it.

A few years prior to our dating, Cory was diagnosed with an astrocytoma, a form of brain cancer. Although she made a strong recovery and all scans indicated the cancer was gone, there may have been a remote possibility of a return. And yet, I relocated us for a career opportunity that I thought was in our best interest without considering one very important aspect: doctors.

Never in a billion years did I think that Cory's brain cancer would return. No one did, not even Cory's doctors. Cory was five years cancer-free, and upon consultation with doctors, they claimed she had successfully beat cancer. She was free to live life and start a family. But then something happened during the pregnancy, and our life's script together changed forever.

Looking back, I often think about the what-ifs and how—despite all the strategic relocation planning discussions—we never once discussed cancer possibilities. How was that even possible? For the life of me, to this day I have no idea how we missed it.

There will always be a part of me that wonders whether—if we hadn't relocated—Cory's primary doctors might have detected the cancer's return earlier through routine doctor appointments, ultimately saving her life. Did the doctors declare her cancer-free too prematurely or provide inaccurate medical advice? I'll never know the answers. Neither will Zoey, nor Cory's family. These unknowns will remain with me for the rest of my life. If there was ever an opportunity to hit that redo button, this might be the one time.

Life is how we grow and learn from decisions. The choices we make enable us to move on. Experiences remind us of the past. Emotions distort the future. What's in between is reality. Facts help us sort that out.

After Cory passed, I felt that love rests with one individual. I couldn't comprehend going through the pain of losing another spouse a second time. It'd be much easier to stay a widower. I was a young, single parent, and my sole focus was Zoey. Plenty of people offered to set me up, but I wasn't interested, and dating wasn't a priority.

Then along came Tracy. We'd known each other since we were babies and even lived just a few houses away from each other for a short period when we were growing up. From our childhood years through graduate school at the University of Arizona, our paths had always crossed. We reconnected again after Cory passed as we lived in the same Chicago suburbs.

At the time, Tracy was a single mother of young twin girls and had gone through a rough patch with her divorce a few years earlier. She understood the difficulty of being a single parent and juggling a career at the same time. Whenever I was in a bind at work or needed help with Zoey, I called Tracy. She would reciprocate at times as well.

I didn't attend support groups to master grief-coping techniques, and I wasn't comfortable sharing my thoughts and feelings with a psychologist. Instead, I confided in Tracy and looked to her for advice, thoughts, and adult companionship.

When many friends disappeared because of the painful memories my presence invoked, Tracy stayed close to me.

After a few years, we began to date as I started taking those little steps. The most challenging moments were at the beginning when I was filled with guilt, as if I were cheating. Even though I knew Cory would have wanted me to move on, we'd never spoken directly about it. I was stuck because I couldn't accept that it was okay. It was very difficult to let go of that notion. But I continued to take steps forward.

They were very little steps, as I truly struggled with each one. For every few steps forward, I took a step backward. The guilt was overpowering, and at times, it affected my relationship with Tracy. Yet, Tracy continued to be patient—she understood me. Although she didn't fully understand what it was like to walk in my shoes, she did her best to listen and be supportive. I give her a lot of credit: it's not easy to date someone who still loves their spouse.

I also felt a certain emptiness inside for Zoey. She didn't have that special mother-daughter bond that other girls her age have, and though she didn't disclose it at first, I could see she yearned for a motherly-type bond. Maybe it was easier for Zoey since she was so young, but she warmed up to Tracy quickly, and together they grew their relationship.

As in any dating relationship, couples experience highs and lows. Withstanding the lows is where the relationship is mostly tested. After nearly five years of dating, I realized that for us to move forward toward marriage, I needed to speak to a professional about the guilt I carried and about how to bring a blended family together successfully.

Eventually, my work with the therapist—combined with taking bigger steps forward—led me to change my perception of getting remarried. Tracy taught me to embrace the mindset that life has much to offer outside of being a widower. I was then in my early 40s, and I'd started to yearn for a lifelong companion, even having a spouse again. Tracy and I were married on October 9, 2016.

Love has no boundaries. It's a passion that burns from the heart. It's up to me to seize life's opportunities, which included remarriage. After all, I wanted to be a better person, a better father, and a better companion.

My experience as a widower molded me differently than my hearing impairment, though it also tasked me to break another label barrier. I had to grow personally to cope with the loss, remove the dating guilt, and eventually let go of barriers entirely. Was it a challenge? Yes. I spent a lot of time asking myself, "What do I truly want in life? Where do I want to go? Who do I want to be?" But as with everything else in my life, I chose not to look in the rearview mirror, only forward.

Your Footsteps

I love using analogies to better explain, which is why I'd like to revisit the jigsaw puzzle for a moment. When constructing a puzzle, sometimes you try to force a piece because you're certain that's where it's supposed to go. But the piece isn't truly a match. Rather than accept it and move on, you begin to justify *why* it should match. You push on it and clench your fist to pat it down, only to pick it up and try again. In the end, you're right back where you started—looking for the right piece all over again. This is what dating felt like!

Try shifting into the dating mindset—let's suppose your partner is a true match. All of the puzzle pieces should align nicely until the very last one is put into place. In dating, that's when you know you want to spend the rest of your life with that person. What makes jigsaw puzzles (and dating partners) so special is that they come in an endless array of themes. After spending vast amounts of energy framing and constructing the puzzle (your relationship), eventually, a masterpiece is presented. This is exactly what dating with the goal of building a meaningful and loving relationship looks like.

We could all share dating horror stories. They're just part of the package deal. I love Jerry Seinfeld's take on it: "What is a date really, but a job interview that lasts all night? The only difference between a date and a job interview is that in not many job interviews is there a chance you'll wind up naked at the end of it."[23]

Looking back, I remember dates that lasted into the morning and were filled with exciting conversations. Believing there was potential, I worked hard to construct the jigsaw puzzle. Sometimes the pieces fit. Other times they didn't.

But what is dating without head-scratching moments? I think the most challenging aspect, by far, are the games that are played. It shouldn't be difficult, yet so much time and energy are lost trying to decipher codes and interpret mixed signals. And these days with the complications of texting and messaging, it's trickier than ever.

And there are those instances when you get the sudden silent treatment: no call or message back, no communication whatsoever, just awkward silence. You either give up or make a complete fool of yourself hanging onto one last thread of hope.

---

23 Jerry Seinfeld, *SeinLanguage* (New York: Bantam Books, 1997), 9.

You might also have experienced the one-and-done type. You had a great time on the first date and expressed an interest in going out again. Then you find out the other person thought the complete opposite or wasn't interested at all. The one-and-done can be tough to swallow. Just when you think you've found your matching puzzle pieces, someone kicks over your puzzle table, forcing you to start all over again.

However, dating has many positive elements too. When you date someone new, not only do you learn whether you're compatible with them, but you also learn a great deal about yourself and what you want in life. With each new date, you discover if another piece fits into your life's jigsaw puzzle. And with all the joys, mishaps, setbacks, confusion, and sudden disappearances that occur in dating, how you react and rebound from each determines whether or not you find the right pieces for assembling your masterpiece.

When you're single without children, dating is a simpler ball game. The focus is on you and the other person because there are fewer scheduling conflicts. Without children, you have more freedom to explore new and endless possibilities without any attachments. There's generally less drama involved.

Dating a divorcée or widow/er is an entirely different ball game. The fact that a previous marriage ended unfavorably can have a dramatic influence on each person's sense of commitment and emotions. It's not an ideal starting point in a dating relationship … but anything is possible!

Sometimes those who come through divorce are more easily able to find new relationships quickly, particularly if the divorce process drags on a for a while, people feel time has been lost, and they're ready to make up for it with a new relationship. There's more of a push to start a new life again and move forward.

A widow/er has a different perception. While some feel the need to fill the void left by their lost loved one immediately, most tend to take their time and are resistant to dating again. The very thought of it is unsettling and upsetting. They may experience the same emotions of guilt that I did. And when the prospect of dating reveals itself down the road one day, movement toward it is as slow as molasses and could take years to materialize.

One of the more controversial widow/er dating topics revolves around photos and personal items left behind by a spouse. On one hand, it's important to respect and preserve the memories and hold onto something tangible. On the other hand, it can be perceived as awkward or intimidating by the new partner. What do you do?

Truthfully, there isn't a right answer as the argument can favor both sides. Instead of weighing the arguments, I recommended doing what you are most comfortable doing, whatever helps you sleep better at night. If your new partner doesn't respect your decision, perhaps they may not be the right fit.

What about dating when there are children involved? It can be challenging because it's not just about the one-to-one match up of you and your date: it's a package deal—with kids. Children come first, because they are the center of the universe for the parent. With scheduling demands and behavioral concerns, the puzzle pieces get more difficult to fit together. And then there's the issue of arranging for a trusted babysitter or nanny on date night. This may not only be a hassle logistically, but it also raises the bar financially. As a result, dates often carry higher expectations, leading to an awkward pressure being felt on either side.

Yes, dating in general is one gigantic jigsaw puzzle, and dating after a marriage has ended is even trickier, but know that going into it. Be sure you're in a good place emotionally, remind yourself not to rush things or try too hard at first. Let the relationship evolve naturally, be grateful for all the things you're going to learn about yourself, and enjoy putting the puzzle together piece by piece.

Our Footsteps

By now, I think we can all agree that dating has a lot of pieces, but there are some clear steps you can take to make the process go more smoothly. If you follow these five steps—or at least some of them—you'll save yourself a lot of time and heartache when constructing your dating puzzle.

1. **KNOW WHAT YOU WANT.**

There are many different forms of dating. It's important to know from the get-go whether you want something casual, serious, or in between. You'll also want to learn your partner's expectations. Remember you're constructing a puzzle and all the pieces have to fit together. If you're looking for something casual and the other person wants a serious relationship, or vice versa, the pieces won't fit no matter how hard you try.

2. **DON'T PLAY GAMES.**

Be open and communicate honestly about the next steps after a date. It's understandable that you might not want to hurt someone's feelings, but being noncommittal makes things worse. Remember that scene in the movie *Swingers,* where Mike has a meltdown when leaving a voice message? It's painful to watch because we've all been there at one point or another. It's okay to express interest before the first date is over. And if the date (or relationship) isn't meeting your expectations, it's also okay to be up-front as to why you don't think it should continue.

3. Be true to who you are.

Be honest with yourself. Remember that you're special because of *who* you are, not *what* you are. Your life story, job, and accomplishments may be fascinating, but those are really about *what* you are. Instead, think about how you want to be perceived by others and share those characteristics with the world. It may be difficult to distinguish between *who* and *what* at first, but if you stay true to yourself, you'll have a better chance of recognizing the *who*.

4. Use the 80/20 rule.

Focus at least 80% of your attention on the qualities of your date that you admire, and never more than 20% of your energy on their less admirable qualities. No one is 100% perfect, and you shouldn't spend your time looking for perfection. Trust your instincts. Compatibility isn't about finding the perfect match but rather cherishing the 80% you admire.

5. Never force a puzzle piece.

Every relationship has challenges, and getting through them makes the relationship stronger. However, if the issue is structural and the pieces simply do not fit, don't force it. You'll just wind up doing more harm than good in the long run.

If it's too difficult in the beginning, most likely it will never work. People don't typically change much over time, so it's unrealistic to expect things will get better down the road. The pieces should easily fit from the get-go, and they should continue to align as you work through the puzzle. A couple that is meant to be can assemble a masterful puzzle even during the bumpiest of times—if the pieces align.

Here are seven steps to help you while dating as a widow/er. These steps also apply if you're dating someone who has previously lost a partner.

1. BE PATIENT AND EMPATHIC.

Burying a spouse is traumatic. The deep void that is left by the loss of your loved one often feels like a hole in your heart. There might come a time when you think you're ready to try a new relationship; however, your own internal conflicts might prevent you from committing. You may even move forward and date someone, only to realize later that you're still not ready.

Remember to be patient and understanding with yourself (and your partner). Deep wounds take time to heal, and everyone heals differently. There's no right or wrong amount of time when a person should feel ready to date again. Eventually, the internal conflicts you've experienced will be replaced with the excitement of a new beginning and a new relationship. I sincerely hope that this book will help you gain this strength.

2. ACCEPT THAT YOU'RE STILL IN LOVE WITH YOUR SPOUSE.

Your previous relationship ended in a tragedy. The fact that you've chosen to move forward with a new relationship doesn't mean that you're going to stop loving your previous spouse or forget about them. You may even draw references from time to time, visit the cemetery, or keep framed pictures nearby. Accept and understand that your spouse and their tragic loss will always mold you into who you are—and that's perfectly natural.

3. STAY IN YOUR OWN MARATHON RACE.

If you're the competitive type who often strives to outdo others, this is not the time. Don't go looking for an exact replica of your late spouse, because that race is over. Instead, begin a new journey by looking for someone who is genuine and engaging, someone who complements you.

4. ACCEPT THERE WILL BE SOME AWKWARD MOMENTS.

Dating after the loss of a spouse is a challenging endeavor.

Like anything that's worth doing in life, if you're making your best effort to move forward, mistakes are going to happen along the way. For example, you might call your new dating partner the wrong name (like the name of your lost spouse). Remember, these mistakes aren't intentional. Forgive yourself, because everyone makes mistakes—especially those who might be particularly vulnerable after a traumatic loss.

5. Introduce your children in due time and with care.

If you're a widow/er with kids, it will probably take you a little time to feel comfortable introducing your child to your new dating partner. As difficult as it is for you to begin a new relationship, children are often even more sensitive when it comes to meeting new people. For example, children may not understand their parents' need for companionship. In their own attempts to make sense of the tragedy and protect themselves from future sorrow, children may consider new dating partners as imminent threats. After all, as their only parent, you're the only one they have left. Naturally, they're going to be scared of losing you too. Give it time, and let your new relationship evolve naturally. Your children will eventually become part of the equation when the time is right.

6. Don't force the marriage issue.

Depending on the type of loss you experienced, and your mental and emotional state, the thought of remarriage may or may not enter your mind. The thought might invoke a strong amount of fear and guilt. However, when you're in the right relationship, those negative emotions will fade. Just as when you began dating your first spouse, stay positive and remain patient. The excitement of remarrying might just reveal itself again, even if it's at a molasses rate!

7. Don't be afraid to seek counseling.

Therapy and grief counseling can be very helpful in processing and learning to live with a traumatic loss. Counseling sessions can also help you get into the right mindset to start dating again when the time is right for you. You've experienced a terrible tragedy, so there's absolutely no shame in seeking professional help and guidance as you try to put the pieces back together.

Self-Reflection Footsteps

Jigsaw puzzles are designed to promote challenge and bring pure enjoyment at the same time. Some puzzles are easier to construct as there are only a few pieces to match, while others take more time and energy. The same can be said for dating. Sometimes it's a natural fit; other times it requires more work to get over some of the primary issues. Understanding the prior relationship of the person you are dating will help explain some of the roadblocks, confusions, or even hesitations.

Dating is about bringing people together and sharing desires and life goals. It's exciting, rewarding, and head scratching all rolled into one. If you are fortunate, when all the pieces finally come together, you're left with a beautiful masterpiece! The following are key summary points, self-guided questions, and self-reflection exercises to help you with dating.

Key Summary Points

1. Dating is one gigantic jigsaw puzzle as the pieces you need to complete are scattered, hard to find, and may not always fit properly.

2. Love has no boundaries. Your heart is big enough for endless, unconditional love.

3. There are definite differences to divorced vs. widow/er dating. Understanding those differences may help you better match the puzzle pieces.

SELF-GUIDED QUESTIONS

1. What do you seek in a companion? Which attributes are most important?

____

____

____

2. How much time and energy do you spend seeking the "perfect" match? What 20% are you willing to let go of?

____

____

____

3. What are the most frustrating aspects in dating? How can you turn those into opportunities?

____

____

____

SELF-REFLECTION EXERCISES

1. Design and create your own jigsaw puzzle.

What characteristics or attributes do you desire in a partner? Perhaps you have a mental list that you keep to check both off-key and admirable traits. Instead of keeping the list in your head, go online to design and create your own jigsaw puzzle. Each piece should represent one of the desires and traits you look for in a partner.

In constructing the actual puzzle, only match the pieces that truly line up with your partner. If a particular piece doesn't match quite yet, that's okay. Give it time. You may be able to match it at a later time. If, after a period, you aren't able to match enough pieces of the puzzle, perhaps your partner is not as good a fit as you once thought. You know the catchphrase "Love is blind"—well, this puzzle may actually be the first tangible way to dispute that notion.

And if all the pieces match and the masterpiece is fully completed, you can frame it as memorabilia or gift it to your partner.

2. Join a widow/er support group as a nonparticipant.

There are many support groups available for widow/ers to discuss grief, dating, and financial distress. If you are dating a widow/er, it may be helpful to attend a group session to listen as a nonparticipant to better comprehend some of the challenges that active participants face. Attending may help you grasp why your dating partner acts, speaks, or responds in certain ways you couldn't entirely understand. The more you can learn and show support, the stronger your relationship will grow. It may just provide another puzzle piece you can match!

To sum it all up, dating isn't easy—especially when you've lost your loved one due to a tragedy and have kids in the mix. It takes a little more preparation (making sure you're ready), a little more humor (to get beyond your rusty dating techniques), and a little more consideration (in understanding your kids' feelings), but it's important that you continue to move forward and explore. Take the time that you need to recover and prepare yourself for the journey. Only you can control, guide the outcome, and *keep those feet moving.*

BOUNCE BACK FROM A JOB LOSS

A job title is nothing more than a bragging right, which is often used to tell others about the superiority of your job that no one else understands but you. Sure, some job titles are more glamorous than others such as vice president, director, or even manager, but truth be told, being gainfully employed is more important than a job title. Unlike paying taxes, employment is not always guaranteed. Unless you are one of the fortunate few, most of us experience job loss at some point in our careers.

My Footsteps

Let's be real: All types of layoffs are hurtful, painful, and demoralizing. In some cases, the emotional scars left behind take years to heal. Your emotional wounds might be so deep that the thought of reliving those moments brings tears to your eyes. I've been laid off more than once, and not a single time has it been pretty. Each instance left behind its own unique scars.

Can you really get laid off on your day off? Yes, you can! Here's what happened. It was July 16, 2001, and I worked for a small boutique advertising company in Chicago. I had been working there for nine months and took my first day off on a Friday as I had friends from college visiting. I arrived at work the following Monday morning, got settled at my desk, and was immediately summoned to the conference room to meet with one of the principals.

Apparently, I'd been let go on Friday due to the downturn in the economy, but no one informed me because, well, I had the day off. No wonder the principals each had ghost looks on their faces when I came through the office doors. No severance, no parting goodbyes, just a simple escort out. My first job as an MBA graduate resulted in a job loss. I was devastated and petrified as I'd relocated from Phoenix to Chicago for the position, only to find myself looking for a new job less than a year later. Just when I thought I was getting my career started, I struggled with limited funds to find my next job.

For the next several months, I took any temporary job I could find—inventory analyst, administrator, it didn't matter—anything for a few dollars in my pocket. Six months later, in January 2002, I landed at a prestigious bank in Chicago as a financial statement analyst, then moved into an anti-money-laundering role. I was at the bank for nearly five years before relocating back to Phoenix to work with my father in accounting. The bank was on the verge of being sold, and I didn't want to go through yet another layoff.

Skipping ahead to April 2009, after Cory was diagnosed with brain cancer for the second time, we relocated back to Chicago where she could be with her family. As difficult as it was to have to give up working with my father, my focus was on Cory. I took an accounting role with a boutique public accounting firm. I'll admit, my work-life balance was absolutely chaotic as I was juggling a full-time work schedule, acting as Cory's caregiver, and raising our daughter. Shortly after Cory passed away, I found myself once again affected by a downturn in the economy and was laid off again. But this time, I wasn't just worried about myself—I had my daughter who depended on me.

Months later, in March 2010, while working at a temporary job as an accounts receivable auditor, the accounting firm helped me secure a controller role with one of their clients. It was the perfect fit—an up-and-coming online media company growing in revenue. I was relieved to start building a stable life for my daughter and myself. But, two and a half years later, in July 2012, the company experienced a downturn, and yet again, I was on the receiving end of another layoff.

"AJ, the company can't afford your salary anymore; we are going to lay you off."

Bad luck or poor choices in finding the right job? Looking back, considering the economy and the situations I was in, I think it was more likely bad luck. However, there was one time I took a position and resigned two months later due to a toxic company culture.

After the online media company, I found a temporary-to-permanent job at a sports marketing company as a controller. Upon starting, I immediately began working nearly 14-hour days to prove to the company owner that I was able to handle the responsibilities of an excessive workload while being a single father. Because I was desperate to support Zoey and myself, I felt compelled to make the best of this employment opportunity. For weeks, my job dictated my schedule, and I worked constantly on time crunches to get all my tasks completed. I couldn't find a good work-life balance, and I felt badly that Zoey was feeling the effects of my long hours.

Then one day Zoey asked me, "Daddy, why don't we play as much as we used to at night?" I didn't have an answer, or at least not one she'd understand.

I fumbled my words, "I know, little girl. You're right."

Right there, that was the turning point. She was absolutely correct. I'd been so consumed by trying to make a living for the two of us that I didn't make enough time for the person who mattered most in my life: Zoey. I resigned from my job and went back to being unemployed.

Luckily, I rebounded quickly and accepted a position at a top fortune 100 insurance company. As glamorous as it was to work for a large company, this one definitely had some drawbacks due to poor leadership and management. In my fourth year with the company, I encountered its deceitful leadership head-on when they conspired to terminate my role because of personal vendettas. When my job was eliminated, I felt beaten down by all the mental, emotional, and verbal engagements with these leaders.

The fallout left me with the belief that I needed to look over my shoulder constantly, especially when it came to my career. At any point, the switch could be flipped, and I could find myself on the receiving end of a layoff discussion or, worse, be set up to fail again. I'll admit, my time at the insurance company left some deep psychological wounds, which are difficult to let go. Although deep down I knew that what happened wasn't the norm, those scars are still with me today.

Since then, I've changed jobs three more times. But the good news is, I left on my own terms as each new job offered better financial and leadership opportunities that aligned with my personal growth and ambition.

When I look back at my career, despite some of the misfortunes, I remind myself just how far I've grown over the years. I've used the negative experiences and career setbacks to work harder, work smarter, and challenge myself to be a better leader. I've learned to appreciate each opportunity I had and strive to be the best I could be.

And should there ever be another time to have the "sit-down," it'll only be a temporary setback. Just as with all the other times, I'll rebound with a better opportunity.

Your Footsteps

Growing up, you have dreams about the type of job you want. You have it all mapped out: what you're going to do, how you're going to get there, how much money you'll make, and all the rest. But by the time you approach the end of high school—depending on your grades—you may find yourself rethinking the future when college becomes a reality.

Some may argue that the name of the school on your college diploma determines what type of career you'll have, but I think it's more about the knowledge and experience you gain over time that has the biggest impact. Success can follow you wherever you decide to go, whether it's working for a large corporation, a small business, or even for yourself. The possibilities are endless—just believe in yourself.

Unfortunately, the chance that you may one day lose your job is part of the reality of being in the workforce. Once you find out the news, you feel as if life has been sucked right out of you. It's painful, it stings, and it's upsetting. You want to run and hide or stay in bed all day and cry it out. It feels as if you've hit rock bottom.

If that isn't enough, there's the agony of endless job applications and interviews, which are enough to drain you mentally and emotionally. The absence of a regular paycheck is terrifying and often results in lost savings, financial cutbacks, and constant anxiety about money. Severance and unemployment insurance might help, if you are lucky enough to get them, but they often don't even cover the bills.

There are many reasons why you might have lost your job. Maybe your company had layoffs. Maybe you were terminated because of something you did. Or maybe you simply needed a change and walked away. Before you can even begin to look for a new job, you need to accept the fact that you are no longer employed. It's a harsh reality check and a difficult concept to come to terms with, but if you don't accept the reality, your emotions will always cloud your ability to move forward in life. Learn to accept your unfortunate situation, and know you won't be unemployed forever. Listen to that voice in your head telling you to wake up, reverse your pattern of behavior, and achieve greater success.

I've learned that there are no jobs greater than protecting the well-being of your health and spending time with your children or loved ones. Keep that in mind, and remember that losing a job and being unemployed are challenges, but they are not permanent fixtures.

A wise man once told me that losing your job doesn't define your career. I didn't understand what he meant at first because I was so caught up emotionally. But once I took some time to think about it further, I realized it really makes sense—losing your job gives you the chance to hit the career restart button all over again. Ask yourself the following questions:

1. What do *you* really want to do?

2. What makes *you* happy?

3. How do *you* want to earn a living?

Take time to think these questions through, as the possibilities are endless! When you are ready to answer them, you'll be able to restart your career. Getting fired or laid off is one of the moments in life when a restart button presents itself. Once the emotional roller coaster ride subsides, you'll be able to see the possibilities ahead. Maybe you'll decide to change careers, take a sabbatical leave to recharge your life, or even retire. Think of it like being reborn.

There will always be battles to face with your health, career, finances, or relationships. How you respond will prove to be the difference between success and further struggles. Sometimes it takes a question like the one that Zoey asked me to put things into perspective, to understand and appreciate all life has to offer. As you continue to build strength each day, realize any fears you are currently facing about job loss are just part of an emotional battle. Seize each day and make the most of whatever opportunity is presented.

Our Footsteps

To help you navigate your career journey, I've segmented this footstep to include the most common phases that you're likely to experience. Each of the four phases is based on my experience with climbing each step to land my next job without compromising my sanity or my mental health.

The Search Phase

If you're out of work or merely searching for a new opportunity, the job-search process can be agonizing. Similar to dating, you're constructing a puzzle. Just what you need is another puzzle, right? Reading over countless job descriptions and spending countless hours on a seemingly endless queue of applications is a full-time job in itself. It's easy to get burned out.

Here are four steps to make the job-search process go smoother and to help you *keep those feet moving* when you're looking for a job.

1. LEVERAGE YOUR LINKEDIN NETWORK.

It's no secret that who you know can make a difference in landing your next job. Reaching out to family and friends alone is not enough. LinkedIn is a valuable tool if used properly, because—unlike other social media platforms—you're able to connect directly with hiring managers, talent acquisition specialists, and virtually anyone else with a profile.

Connecting with the right people and networking groups can facilitate your job search: You'll have allies helping you get your foot in the door of their company or their network. By leveraging networks, you'll open doors to new horizons that you never knew existed.

2. DON'T APPLY TO NEWLY POSTED JOBS.

There's a general perception that the first few applicants for new job postings are more likely to secure an interview. The issue is that hiring managers are often overwhelmed by the initial flood of applications, so it's impossible for them to get a good glimpse of your unique skill set. As a result, your chances of being selected from among the initial horde of applicants are low.

Instead, wait until the job posting is at least four weeks old. By then, hiring managers might be less critical of your résumé and more eager to fill the open seat. Your chance of getting a better salary might also go up because the position is still vacant. To sum it up, applying to older job postings often leads to a less intense interview process and maybe even a higher salary.

3. Use word clouds.

Word clouds have proved to be an invaluable tool for highlighting keywords in a textual data visualization, allowing you to see which words have the highest frequency within a given body of text. If you haven't used a word cloud, trust me, it will make a difference in your next job application!

Here's how it works: Copy the job description into a word cloud to identify and highlight key words. The bolder the word, the greater its importance and frequency in the job description. Now copy your résumé into the same word cloud. Do your keywords match the job description's keywords? If so, you have a high probability of getting through the initial computer screening as the system looks for keywords. If you *don't* find keywords matching, modify your résumé to include the keywords and repeat the process. Still not matching? It may be because you aren't the right fit. Instead focus on those jobs that better match your qualifications and skills.

4. Job search at night.

Finding a new job is a full-time job, but who says you have to spend your whole day searching? Have you noticed that when you spend all day at your computer completing endless applications, it often seems that the call backs or email responses you're hoping for never come? Why is that? It's because you're expecting something to magically happen.

Conversely, it often seems that when you're out visiting friends, running errands, enjoying your favorite hobby, or getting exercise, your day gets interrupted with job-related phone calls and emails. This is why you should search for jobs at night when all is calm. You'll then give yourself the rare opportunity to do the nonwork-related things you want to do during the day. Taking this approach, you'll soon discover that job searching isn't so bad after all!

The Hiring Phase

If you ask me, the hiring process is flawed. Applicants are asked to take time away from their current roles or commute long distances for a brief in-person discussion. If the first interview is successful, there's sure to be another round, which means more challenges as the second interview may be longer and applicants are *again* asked to take time away and commute. Worst of all, by the time the interviewing process is over, there's still the chance that you won't be selected for the position. Now you're back to square one, with only more disappointment and frustration to show for it. What if there was an easier way? There is.

Here are three steps to help you *keep those feet moving* during the hiring process and knock your interviews out of the park.

1. BOOST YOUR CONFIDENCE WITH PREPARATION.

Being confident during an interview is a surefire way to increase your chances of getting hired. But you can't be confident if you're not prepared. This is why I recommend overpreparing for the interview. Study—in detail—the job description, company history, the industry, and the interviewers' backgrounds, and prepare answers for dozens of potential interview questions. Any information you learn about the company before the interview might give you a competitive edge. When you're well prepared, your confidence rises, making it easier for you to articulate why you're the best applicant for the job.

2. LEVERAGE YOUR SKILL SET.

You offer an exceptional and unique skill set, so sell it! Tell the story of *who you are*, not what you do. There's a genuine difference. The *who* aspect demonstrates your value and how your skills align with the company's needs. This is what makes you shine. The *what* aspect merely summarizes your career and explains what tasks you can perform. Of the two, which do you think a hiring manager or potential coworker would be more excited about?

3. CLOSE STRONG.

Remember that it's not where you start that matters so much— it's how you finish that leaves a lasting impression. Summarize the key takeaways concisely and with a smile. Yes, a smile. Smiling shows confidence and credibility, and it makes you more relatable. Most hiring managers interview multiple applicants consecutively, so give yourself the advantage.

Also, don't forget to give a firm handshake and express sincere interest in the next steps. Last, follow up with a concise thank-you note. These subtle elements complement each other to build a strong close. More importantly, they increase your odds of getting hired!

The Missed Job-Promotions Phase

Job promotions are usually based on accomplishments, recognitions, and rewards. They also show that the company is invested in you and that leaders believe you're a key performer. Depending on your career goals, promotions can be significant stepping-stones to a larger role within the company. Unfortunately, landing a promotion is harder to do today than it used to be.

Think about it from a manager's perspective. If you excel in your role, your manager doesn't have to worry about your work. If you're promoted, your manager now has to find your replacement. And once your replacement is trained, they might not do as good a job as you. Could this be a reason why managers often don't promote employees? Perhaps. Or they'd rather risk that you won't leave for another opportunity.

This is exactly what happened to me. In one situation, after receiving a stellar performance review, I was excited about potentially getting a promotion for an open position that I thought I was perfectly qualified for. At last, all the extra work that I had put into completing challenging projects and meeting deadlines would be worth it—or so I thought. A few days later when I was called in for a meeting with my manager, I was brimming with excitement about the good news I was expecting to hear.

Much to my dismay, instead of a promotion, my manager told me there was a team restructure. The promotion I hoped for was given to another colleague, who had been at the company only a short time. Adding insult to injury, I now had to report to this person.

When I tried to get an explanation as to why I was passed over, my manager fumbled to come up with any sort of reasonable answer. It was a truly disheartening conversation that changed my perception of the company and the dynamic of my manager's leadership. So, what did I do? Because of the lack of promotions and growth opportunities, I left the company two months later for a much better job. Instead of feeling dejected, I took immediate action and made a positive change.

Here are three steps to help you *keep those feet moving* if you're overlooked for a promotion.

1. SAVE THE EMOTIONAL OUTBURST.

Deep down inside, you probably want to yell curse words at your manager, or even worse! You may even be so overwhelmed with emotion that you're on the verge of a breakdown. Before you do *anything*, count backward in your head from 10 to zero. That moment of silence will help you process what's been said. You'll then be able to handle the news gracefully and politely excuse yourself without offending anyone or damaging your reputation. Then take a few more minutes to breathe and refocus. If possible, reserve any emotional outbursts or complaints for a discussion with a friend or loved one after you leave work.

2. DON'T RUSH TO ANY DECISIONS.

When you're passed up for a promotion, it can be difficult to rebound in your current role. Whether it's due to embarrassment or extreme disappointment, your confidence may be shattered, and you may also have a genuine lack of trust in the leadership. In these instances, it's easy to throw in the towel and announce that you're quitting. Or you may decide to do the bare minimum of work as an act of defiance.

Although these choices might be understandable, the issue is that they mean you're making impulse decisions based on emotions. I hope you've learned by now that emotions cloud your judgment and block your ability to logically process situations. Instead, keep the faith; there might be something bigger behind the scenes you can't yet see. Wait a few days, or even weeks, before you make any career-related decisions. Once your emotions subside, you'll have a clearer vision of your career.

3. TAKE STEPS FORWARD.

There's no need to concentrate any further on the missed promotion. It's behind you. To continue agonizing over it will only delay the bright vision ahead of you. And the sad truth is, after a few days, no one will want to hear about it anymore. As difficult as it is to move forward, it's something you have to do. Everything happens for a reason: It may not be clear at first, you might not like it or understand it initially, but remember, there's a bigger picture ahead. If you look forward with optimism and positivity, it'll soon come to light. Taking those steps forward will set you on the right path to get there.

The Laid Off or Fired Phase

Be mindful of the fact that getting laid off or fired can be extremely traumatizing. Some people may become so overwhelmed emotionally that they are unable to conceive of the idea that in a few days, or in a week, their life might start to look pretty good again—especially once the restart button is pressed!

Here are three steps for you to *keep those feet moving* if you've been laid off or fired.

1. SLOWLY LET GO.

It's natural to rewind the sequence of events that led to the layoff or firing in your mind and ask yourself, "Could this have been avoided? Why didn't I see this coming?" Or you may think, "I knew it was coming, but I thought I could survive it."

During the first few days, it's normal to experience emotional ups and downs. You'll likely feel a mix of rejection, sadness, and perhaps even anger. Soon after, it's time to start letting it go because that chapter in your life has finished. No, it wasn't a pretty ending, but that chapter will remain closed now, so you can move on.

2. ESTABLISH A NEW ROUTINE.

One benefit of a layoff or firing is that it forces you to establish a new routine. It is the perfect opportunity to introduce a new way of doing things, declutter, and get rid of old habits that don't provide personal value or positive results. You're beginning a new chapter in your life—write a good one!

3. GET SOME SUNSHINE.

It's amazing how quickly sunshine can brighten your mood. When you go from darkness to light, the warmth of the sun instantly puts you at ease. If you're feeling down, make a point of spending more time outdoors than you normally would. If getting outside isn't an option, try to position yourself near windows where the sun shines through. You'll be amazed at how quickly the sun will help clear your vision of the path ahead.

Self-Reflection Footsteps

Your days are filled with enough anxiety, stress, and uncertainty as it is. Coupled with job losses, illnesses, broken relationships, or financial distress, it's no surprise that, by the end of the day, you've reached your resistance point. While you may never be truly prepared for setbacks and challenges, you do have the opportunity to alter your perceptions to overcome any adversity that arises. Below are key summary points, self-guided questions, and a self-reflection exercise to help you with job loss.

KEY SUMMARY POINTS

1. Job loss is only a temporary setback. You will rebound into a better opportunity.

2. There are no jobs greater than protecting the well-being of your health and spending time with your children or loved ones.

3. Losing your job doesn't define your career—it's a chance to hit the career restart button.

SELF-GUIDED QUESTIONS

1. How much of an emotional toll has your job or career taken on your mental health? What could you do differently to strengthen your work-life balance?

____

____

____

2. How often do you sacrifice family time or other important events because you've placed your previous job on a higher pedestal? What opportunities were missed that you regretted?

____

____

____

3. What does the restart button look like for you? What's stopping you from getting your ideal job?

____

____

____

SELF-REFLECTION EXERCISES

1. Refocus your energy.

It all starts with you and your ability to control your thoughts. Empower yourself to put aside any negativity and focus your energy on what you can control. Repetition, encouragement, and belief are all factors that can help you rise up. While job losses can be devastating to your morale, simply saying words of encouragement aloud can be quite empowering.

I am who I am.
I am strong.
I am fearless.
I am beautiful.
I am intelligent.
I am blessed.
I am free.
I am thankful.
I am happy.
I will overcome challenges.
I will laugh and smile.
I will write my own story.
I will stand tall.
I will find a way or make one.
I will push myself to new limits.
I will climb mountains.
I will inspire others to follow.
I will seize the day.
I will change the world.
I will take back control of my life.
I will live my life as I want to.

Inspiring stories, motivation techniques, and empowering words truthfully can only move your feet a few steps forward. The steps afterward are determined by your strength, willpower, and perceptions.

Go ahead and self-reflect. Think about the type of life you want. What does that look like? How would it feel? Self-reflection helps you remove the unwanted clutter and place balance back in your life once again. It's all about who you are and how you decide to *keep those feet moving*.

8

CLIMB INTO A RENEWED FAITH

I've tended to shy away from religious topics out of respect for the wide range of opinions and beliefs out there. The subject was controversial when I was growing up, and it remains controversial today. Depending on how you were raised or what shaped your viewpoints through the years, your religion—your faith—is a vital part of who you are today.

In 2017, I reconnected with my faith, which revolutionized me to embrace and open my heart to my religion once again. I feel compelled to share my experience because finding faith might just help you too.

My Footsteps

When I was growing up, religion wasn't much of a focal point in my household. My parents did their best to introduce Judaism by celebrating certain holidays and adhering to certain traditions, but that was really the extent of our Judaic practices at that time.

By 1984, when I was nine, my parents thought it was time for me to join a community synagogue in an effort to further my Judaic studies. Unfortunately, the studies felt more like an obligation—Saturday mornings, from a youngster's perspective, did not feel like the ideal time to go to school to learn. The same hearing impairment insecurities that I faced at grammar school followed me to Saturday school and later to Hebrew and Sunday schools.

Despite my hearing impairment, I learned to speak and read beginner Hebrew. Based on memorization and recitations, the language lessons were focused more on learning prayers than on conversational Hebrew. Had the teachings been more conversational, perhaps I would have been more intrigued and would have continued my Judaic studies post middle school and better observed the Judaic traditions in my early adulthood.

Through my early years, I learned that religion is one's interpretation of divine will and that faith is your acceptance of and relationship with that will. While the teachings delved into a deeper understanding of the religion itself, there wasn't a lot of significance put on the aspect of faith.

I began to lose my faith in my early adulthood because of the numerous personal setbacks I endured. I struggled to understand why I was born with a hearing impairment, yearned for social acceptance, and suffered from panic attacks. If you also include the heartaches and pain of the job losses and the financial challenges that followed, it's no surprise that I naturally questioned how it was possible for one person to experience one setback after another. Why did I constantly struggle to get through life? Why couldn't I catch a break? As I continued to lose faith, I focused more on the "why me?" aspect.

The final punch was when Cory was diagnosed with terminal brain cancer and my constant prayers for a cure went unanswered. Throughout those days, I prayed for a miracle. I spent nights in solitude asking for forgiveness for any wrongdoings. I recited scriptures from memory. I pleaded and offered restitutions. I even took Cory to see a Reiki master for spiritual healing. I did everything I could through prayer to help Cory fight her battle. For 14 months, this went on as part of my daily routine. Despite the grim reports, I continued to press harder on prayers. The evening when Cory passed, I was in despair and completely gave up hope because I was angry and confused. I was lost within my faith and accepted the fact that my life would always be a constant struggle.

For eight years, my faith remained relatively dormant. It wasn't until I journeyed on a MoMENtum Men's Trip to Israel that I was able to fully comprehend the power of faith and prayer. Little did I know that something bigger was around the corner.

Taglit-Birthright Israel and MoMENtum trips are partially subsidized by Jewish organizations and the Israeli government as an opportunity for Jewish adults to journey through Israel to experience a deeper connection with Judaism and explore places and history that shaped their Jewish identity.

In 2015, Tracy participated in a life-changing MOMentum Women's Trip to Israel and returned with a renewed appreciation of faith and spirituality. At the time she went, I didn't comprehend the significance nor understand the trip's impact on her. In an effort to help me better understand, she later introduced me to Rabbi David, the husband of the woman who led Tracy's group. As it turned, I was drawn to Rabbi David as his teachings immediately resonated with me.

Two years later, in 2017, Rabbi David recruited a group of men for a MoMENtum Men's Trip to Israel. It was designed to be a similar experience to Tracy's, but this trip predicated more on teachings to inspire men to connect deeply with their Jewish heritage and to transform themselves, their families, and ultimately their communities. The trip included an eight-day adventure to Israel, stretching from the mystical Galilee city of Tzfat to the ancient desert mountaintop fortress of Masada.

Tracy saw this as a great opportunity for me to reconnect with my faith and immediately signed me up. I don't recall whether we actually had an in-depth discussion. I think it was more like, "You're going. You need this for yourself!"

Still, I wasn't fully on board and had my own reservations about the overall experience, but both Rabbi David and Tracy helped me embrace the opportunity ahead. If any faith was out there, it certainly wasn't attached to anything that I could grab onto at that time.

As fate would have it, I was among 15 men selected by Rabbi David for this incredible trip. Unlike some of the guys who knew each other from prior encounters, I didn't know any of them. I was a bit outside my comfort zone.

In the months and weeks that led up to the trip, each of the other men spoke about his thoughts, skepticism, and curiosity about what was to come. For some, including me, this would be a first trip to Israel. Some of us had clear goals in mind, while others were going because their wives encouraged them to go based on their own positive experiences.

When the day to depart finally arrived, I was clueless about what to expect when I arrived in Israel. As soon as I landed, I found myself looking for a sign, any sign. But of what? I had no idea what I was looking for or what I was doing. Was I supposed to feel radically different? Would some overpowering image suddenly appear to guide me?

Two days later, smack-dab in the middle of the Judean Desert, it all came together. We were on a group hike up the Masada path, which is known for its historical significance and endurance-testing terrain. It was extremely hot, and I was almost out of water, dripping in sweat.

All of a sudden, I felt a transformation. I didn't think anything of it at first, but as I continued to ascend the path, the feeling grew stronger and stronger. With each step, I felt strong sensations going in and out of my body, as if I was having out-of-body experiences.

As I climbed the final section, I caught up to one of the guys from my group, and we congratulated each other on completing the grueling journey. Then, when I had a moment to myself, I stood at the railing looking down 1,300 meters over the Dead Sea, trying to take in the experience. That's when it occurred to me that those strange bodily sensations were my faith being restored. Hiking the Masada was a life-changing moment for me. It'll be forever designated as the place where I found faith again.

I experienced spirituality a day later at the Kotel, which is an ancient limestone prayer wall in Jerusalem's Old City. Prior to walking to the Kotel, 200-plus men stood in the Aish Center foyer overlooking the Western Wall, listening to the most intense, powerful, inspiring speech given by our MoMENtum leader. Within his speech, he spoke about how many of our male ancestors never had the chance to experience what we were about to experience. We were there for a divine purpose, and our lives would forever change. He concluded his speech by encouraging us to walk out from the Aish Center to the Kotel in complete silence, just taking in the entire experience. The five-minute walk in silence was a prelude to what I was about to experience next.

The power you feel at the Kotel is very real. It's a force unlike anything else I've ever experienced. Unless you've been there, it's difficult to put the emotional feeling that consumes you at the wall into context.

Although I've never been one to be emotional, tears ran down my face as I prayed at the wall. I had much to pray for and to be thankful for. The Kotel overpowered me as I released emotions, thoughts, and feelings. For the first time in my life, I felt faith and spirituality together. I was home.

It wasn't until I rediscovered my faith and spirituality that I was able to understand why my prayers from earlier in my life went unanswered. It was because I was praying incorrectly. Instead of offering praise and gratitude, I was merely praying about my current situation and dictating wishes.

Since my Israel trip, on multiple occasions, I've seen the greatness of the Almighty through the power of prayer. From two career opportunities to a recent health scare, none of the outcomes could have been accomplished without the blessing of the Almighty. Instead of praying and placing stipulations, I simply thanked Him and turned everything over to Him in faith.

Every day I am blessed. All the setbacks I've experienced were part of a divine plan for the Almighty to do work in me. I may not have understood at the time, but I do now. Each day I awake, I believe I've been given a new opportunity to honor the Almighty. Throughout each day I say thank you and look for His signs pointing me in the right direction. I've also learned to trust my faith and to be a blessing for others. Even when I don't see a way or understand, I stay in faith.

What's amazing to me is that my spiritual transformation in Israel changed not only my perception of prayer, but it also changed my understanding of my life's purpose, my hearing impairment, and all those setbacks.

Everything in life happens for a reason. Often it cannot be explained in words or make sense. Sometimes you have to trust faith to guide you through troubled times. It took 15 guys and a rabbi to form a brotherhood bond for me to find faith and spirituality. And for that, I thank each of those 15 guys, Rabbi David, and especially Tracy for encouraging me to go on the MoMENtum Men's Trip.

These guys were previously strangers to me, but I now share an unbreakable bond with them that I will forever cherish. And in case you're wondering, there's a core group of us that remains closely knit today.

Your Footsteps

Have you ever noticed that life resembles a Rubik's Cube? Each color represents different concerns of importance, such as religion, faith, spirituality, health, relationships, and finances. No matter which way you turn the cube, colors become integrated, sometimes without any real logic. Just when you think you made all the right turns, you discover that the colors are further scrambled, but as you continue to turn the cube, you begin to notice how to bring those concerns together one by one.

Rubik's Cubes come in different sizes, shapes, and forms, and—much like your life's challenges—not all of them move in the same direction. You may have to improvise as you think about the direction of each turn. Despite the difficulty, you have to keep turning.

There are moments in life when it is just easier to toss the Rubik's Cube away. The odds against you are overwhelming. The agony of continuing is too great, and the desire to continue on may be lost. But before you give up, ask yourself one question: "Have I truly done everything I could to overcome the challenges I face?"

As I've said throughout these pages, you have the power to overcome the obstacles you face. You have the power to knock down barriers that stand in your way. You have the ability to rewrite fate and direct it. It all starts with your perception and your game plan for success. It won't come easy. It'll take time and patience. There will be moments of frustration and barriers that you encounter. But if you stay with it and keep turning, eventually you'll see how all the colors come together. Fate doesn't control that Rubik's Cube—you do.

Solving my own Rubik's Cube was a great personal accomplishment. Looking back at the battles I fought and the pain of life's punches, I realize that all that I've endured over my lifetime has led me to the life I lead today. The experiences gained propelled me to climb the Masada to rediscover my faith, to visit the Kotel to feel the intense power of prayer, and ultimately to overcome various obstacles related to my hearing impairment, loss of a spouse, and job losses.

I've been fortunate at times and blessed with opportunities over the years, and I understand that not everyone has the same outlook when it comes to family values, religious upbringing, and faith. Your past experiences have led you this far along your life's journey. Whether you are ready to recognize that in your own life depends on your faith and comfort zone.

Your comfort zone protects you from harm, providing security, confidence, and contentment. Over time, in facing any unfavorable or unforeseen challenges, you may quickly isolate yourself and immediately retreat to your comfort zone for survival. In a sense, your comfort zone acts as a place for peace and harmony—much like your faith. Often, life experiences and fears will shuffle you in and out of your comfort zone, sometimes tempting you to step out when you might not be ready. In some instances, you may find yourself missing out on new opportunities, opting for comfort instead. But what happens when your comfort zone suddenly becomes a personal barrier?

There are always trade-offs in life. You want to make more money but not switch jobs. You want a clean bill of health, but you elect not to take proper care of yourself. You want to go out with friends for an evening but choose to relax at home after a long day. Rarely does the opportunity present itself in which you can have it all. Alternatively, you come to the conclusion that something has got to give.

How many opportunities have you lost by staying within the confines of your comfort zone? How many times have you wished you had reacted differently and had taken the opportunity presented? We've all been there. The past can't be changed, but the future hasn't been fully written yet either.

As you age, your faith and comfort zone generally define you. That may be a reason why you aren't further along in your career, recovery, or life. You use your comfort zone as an excuse for your actions or inaction. Why? Because it's simply easier than putting forth the effort.

What are you afraid of? Failure? Disappointment? Ridicule? Perhaps a combination of all of them. But you can't go through life shielding yourself within the confines of your comfort zone. You will never overcome those barriers you face; you will never pride yourself on knowing that you have an opportunity to lead a better, more enriched life.

The next time you are presented an opportunity, accept it, and break free from your comfort zone even if you feel lost, insecure, or scared. The most important thing is that you take the initiative. Grow confidence. Act as if. Change your perception. Step into a new zone. Think about it: Which is worse, stepping outside your comfort zone, or missing out on new opportunities to enhance your life? Yes, there are trade-offs, but isn't that what living is all about?

Although they are intertwined, faith doesn't always have to be about religion. It's about building trust or confidence in someone or something. It can be devotion or passion for something you truly care about and believe in. It can be anything that inspires or motivates you.

Do you remember when the actress Jane Fonda coined the phrase "no pain, no gain?" You still hear it all the time. The phrase relates to how toughness is 99% of a mental battle. Whether you're at the gym, dealing with a work situation, or navigating an emotional challenge, failure is caused not because you lack physical strength but because you lack the mental conditioning needed to succeed.

In sports, people talk about getting into a zone. Some of you may be familiar with it: When you are in the zone, it's not your body that propels you; it's your motivation, focus, and mental commitment. Think about the goals you set in your life, the standards you abide by. It's your perceptions that dictate whether you succeed or not. Strength comes from within, and your toughness builds on itself over time. Faith does this too!

The story of Michael Jordan is well known. He could have easily walked away after being cut from his high school basketball team. Instead, he used it as motivation to propel himself to become what I believe is the best basketball player to ever play.

Businessman and motivational speaker Chris Gardner was homeless for nearly one year, struggling to make ends meet when he took an internship opportunity with the stock brokerage firm Dean Witter Reynolds. Despite his financial struggles, he never revealed to colleagues his dire situation. His determination to live a better life for himself and his son enabled him to turn the internship opportunity into a full-time job, which in turn led him to form his own multimillion-dollar brokerage firm.

Bethany Hamilton was a competitive surfer beginning at a young age. When she was 13 years old, she was attacked by a shark that severed her left arm. One month later, she was back on the surfboard competing. Relying on her strength and positive spirit, she went on to win first place in the Explorer Women's Division of the National Scholastic Surfing Association National Championships.

There are many more stories out there, including stories that haven't been written or told yet. Now's the opportunity to have your story written.

In some capacity, faith is needed to help propel you to the next level. It can be your inner drive to overcome an illness, a personal challenge or crisis, or simply a sports-related competition. Whatever your goal may be, find faith to jump-start your motivation for getting there. Sometimes you may only have one moment, one small window of opportunity. Are you ready?

Remember those curveballs? Curveballs are designed to throw you off, to knock you out of your game. Although many consider curveballs something to avoid, use them to your advantage as a form of motivation to strengthen your faith. Instead of stepping away, step up to it. Take those chances. Take those risks. If you don't step up to face your challenges now, when will you? After the fact, when it's too late?

Believe you will succeed. Trust your faith, and let it guide you in moments when and where you need it most, no matter what curveballs life throws at you or how difficult your Rubik's Cube may be.

Our Footsteps

When you lose faith, feelings of emptiness and loneliness typically follow. There's an unnatural buildup of resentment or despair that weighs heavily in your heart and soul. Fortunately, with a little openness and perhaps fate, it can be rediscovered. Whether you look for faith or it comes to you instantaneously, there's an aura of tranquility that surrounds you once faith is found again.

Below are three steps to help you *keep those feet moving* when you've lost your faith.

1. SEEK GUIDANCE.

Depending on your religion, faith, and spirituality, you may benefit from speaking to someone who you identify as a model for your faith. It may be anyone—with or without a religious designation—whom you can confide in to help guide you. Some people may deem seeking guidance a sign of weakness, but in reality, it's a sign of strength. No one can walk in your shoes and truly comprehend how you feel, but seeking guidance may help your faith return.

2. FIND YOUR PASSION.

What are you truly passionate about? It may be something related to your religion, a philanthropic cause, or a goal you seek. It could be an individual whose words inspire or motivate you to do more. Perhaps it's a reading or passage of influence. It could be places or surroundings that hold great significance. Use that passion to help drive your faith.

3. PRAY.

The power of prayer can be very emotional as you express thoughts and feelings, ask for forgiveness and repentance, or simply engage. When you pray, there's no need to belong to or believe in a particular religion. Just have a direct conversation with a higher power. The beauty of prayer is that it can be anything you want to share. Speak internally, aloud, chant—it doesn't matter as there are no rules. Some people may quote scripture; others may speak more freely.

What's most important to understand is that not all prayers will be answered immediately, and in some instances, they may never be answered. This is when faith ultimately gets tested. But if you continue to pray and stay in faith, those prayers just one day may be answered.

Self-Reflection Footsteps

There was a time when you once believed in something, maybe even prayed with the hope of it coming true. Think about the circumstances of your request and why you felt prayer was important. Were your prayers answered?

Again, faith doesn't always have to be about religion and prayer. It's more about the passion and beliefs that you carry. While "Our Footsteps" provided starter steps, below are key summary points, self-guided questions, and self-reflection exercises to help you find faith.

KEY SUMMARY POINTS

1. Everything in life happens for a reason. Sometimes you have to trust faith to guide you through troubled times.

2. Faith is not always about religion; it's about building trust or confidence in someone or something.

3. Failure is caused not because you lack physical strength but because you lack the mental conditioning needed to succeed.

SELF-GUIDED QUESTIONS

1. How can you solve your own Rubik's Cube? What six elements represented are most important to you?

____

____

____

2. What are you passionate about? Where do you draw inspiration and motivation?

____

____

____

3. How has faith guided you in challenging situations? What did you learn from the experience?

____

____

____

Self-Reflection Exercises

1. Accept your past with blessings.

Your past cannot be undone; your experiences are part of who you are today. Too often, painful experiences are held on to because it's easier to accept them for what they were rather than to let them go. The longer you hold onto those experiences, the greater your faith is negatively affected. To help alleviate the tension associated with your past, you need to face the reality that certain painful memories are no longer welcome. Faith is to be restored!

Before you take a step forward, you must first accept your past. As difficult as it may be, I find writing to be quite therapeutic and a great documentation source, especially for capturing thoughts and feelings. Lists can sometimes be more helpful than diaries as you can check off lines one by one. Using a sheet of paper or a spiral notebook, write down as many experiences as you can remember where you may have prayed for a more favorable outcome. Place a checkmark next to each experience that left a profound impact. Looking at the checkmarks, write two blessings that resulted from the experience. Use those blessings to slowly transform those profound experiences into faith. As you continue through the exercise, hopefully you'll gain a new perspective that for every painful experience, two blessings will soon follow.

2. Meditate.

Meditation offers many benefits that can significantly help you, especially when you're looking to bring tranquility and peace back into your life. It's about finding the inner balance and harmony to guide you through self-discovery. By incorporating meditation into your routine—depending on your spirituality and meditation preferences—you may find faith flowing through you sooner than you expected.

3. Go on a birthright trip.

Birthright trips offer amazing experiences to help you connect with your religion, faith, and spirituality. Most programs are subsidized to allow participants to enjoy various programs that best align with their needs, goals, and interests. Some programs may be more religious and faith-based than others—not all programs are alike.

Before deciding on a birthright trip, think about the type of trip and experience you want. Think about what you want to gain and—most importantly—whether what the trip offers lines up with your personal values and expectations. Then find a birthright trip that meets your criteria. It can seem overwhelming at first, but once you make your selection, it becomes not only exciting but life changing!

Here are several birthright trips you might want to explore: Taglit-Birthright Israel, Heritage Greece, ReConnect Hungary, Birthright Macedonia, Birthright Armenia, Tu Cuba, and Global Irish Summer Camp.

My writings are a direct reflection of empathy, compassion, and understanding of what inspires and motivates people. Life is not about being popular or how many friends you have. It's not about how much money you have or fancy possessions. It's about accepting yourself for who you are. It's about giving back to those in need. It's about living each moment to its fullest extent without regrets, fears, or pain. Too often we look at our past as indicators of the future. But what we thought we knew back then couldn't be more different from what we know now.

We all experience many setbacks, but with the right perception, none of them change who we are for the worse. Instead, they make us stronger, smarter, and more appreciative of what we have. We still have to make mistakes and get our tongues tied into knots. However, those things won't take away how far we've come.

No one said it would be easy. Then again, you never asked for it to be easy. Life lessons are blessings in disguise. What you take away from them makes them that much more special. I think faith has a lot to do with that.

> **This is your time; it doesn't matter where you started or where you're at right now. What matters most is how you take those next steps forward and to *keep those feet moving.***

ACKNOWLEDGMENTS

I cannot express enough gratitude and appreciation to all those who've supported "Keep Those Feet Moving" since its launch in 2013. It's truly heart-warming to see how my blog has impacted and touched the lives of many. This book shares a more in-depth perspective into my life, which enables me to open up and better connect to readers.

With that said, this book could not have been possible without Ian Brennan, my mentor and friend, who encouraged me to share my story. Not just an overview of my story, but to peel back the hidden layers to delve deeper into who I am, my thoughts and feelings, and more importantly, accepting how my past shaped the person I am today.

The completion of this book could not have been accomplished without the guidance and expertise of Julie Broad and her team at Book Launchers. I was fortunate to work with an amazing team who challenged me to find my voice and structure the book.

And to my wife, Tracy Coleman, thank you for your love and support. You've always helped me through tough times and brought comfort during the darkest moments. You are an integral part of my life, and I appreciate all you've done for Zoey and me.

… And to Cory Coleman, I am eternally blessed for how you touched my life and the legacy you left behind for Zoey and me. You've been our angel watching over us, guiding us through your love. You are missed each day and forever in our hearts.